THE PANIZZI LECTURES
1998

Previously published Panizzi Lectures

BIBLIOGRAPHY AND THE SOCIOLOGY OF TEXTS
by D. F. McKenzie (*1985*)

ENGLISH MONARCHS AND THEIR BOOKS
by T. A. Birrell (*1986*)

A NATIONAL LIBRARY IN THEORY AND IN PRACTICE
by K. W. Humphreys (*1987*)

DAPHNIS AND CHLOE:
THE MARKETS AND METAMORPHOSES OF AN UNKNOWN BESTSELLER
by Giles Barber (*1988*)

THE DUTCH AND THEIR BOOKS IN THE MANUSCRIPT AGE
by J. P. Gumbert (*1989*)

ERASMUS, COLET AND MORE:
THE EARLY TUDOR HUMANISTS AND THEIR BOOKS
by J. B. Trapp (*1990*)

THE ENGLISH BOOK IN EIGHTEENTH-CENTURY GERMANY
by Bernhard Fabian (*1991*)

HEBREW MANUSCRIPTS OF EAST AND WEST:
TOWARDS A COMPARATIVE CODICOLOGY
by Malachi Beit-Arié (*1992*)

THE MANUSCRIPT LIBRARY OF SIR ROBERT COTTON
by Colin Tite (*1993*)

MUSIC, PRINT AND CULTURE IN EARLY SIXTEENTH-CENTURY ITALY
by Iain Fenlon (*1994*)

MAPS AS PRINTS IN THE ITALIAN RENAISSANCE
by David Woodward (*1995*)

THE INTRODUCTION OF ARABIC LEARNING INTO ENGLAND
by Charles Burnett (*1996*)

THE HISTORY OF BOOKBINDING AS A MIRROR OF SOCIETY
by Mirjam M. Foot (*1997*)

The Panizzi Lectures
1998

Publishing Drama
in Early Modern Europe

ROGER CHARTIER

THE BRITISH LIBRARY

First published 1999 by
The British Library
96 Euston Road
St Pancras
London NW1 2DB

Cataloguing in Publication Data
A catalogue record for this title is
available from The British Library

ISBN 0 7123 4635 X

Designed by John Mitchell
Typeset by Bexhill Phototypesetters, Bexhill-on-Sea
Printed in England by Henry Ling (Printers) Ltd,
Dorchester

Contents

For Marta

Acknowledgements

I WOULD LIKE TO thank Stephen Parkin for his excellent organization of this series of lectures delivered at the British Library on December 8th, 9th and 10th, 1998. I would also like to thank him and Kathleen Houghton for having carefully perused my text and for having taught, in the words of Thomas Heywood (used in other circumstances), my lame English to walk 'upright upon its feete'.

Preface

DECEMBER 1998. Don McKenzie was sitting in the front row of the auditorium of the British Library where I gave the three lectures contained in this little book. My memory of him is always linked to the image of this smiling and kindly presence.

Nearly fifteen years earlier, in this same British Library, he inaugurated the 'Panizzi Lectures in Bibliography' with a series of lectures which made an exceptional intellectual impact. Published under the title of 'Bibliography and the sociology of texts', and translated into French, Italian, and (imminently) into Spanish, they proposed a new research perspective which linked closely the production, transmission and reception of texts, whatever their nature and medium.

In order to reconstruct the process of the publication of works, and their conditions of appropriation, McKenzie gave pride of place to an analysis of the material forms of texts. But in calling his approach a 'sociology of texts', he showed that the description of manuscript or printed objects could be separated neither from the critical analysis of the works, nor from the history of readers and reading. For numerous scholars, coming from unrelated, and even conflicting disciplines, this programme offered the promise of a richer, denser understanding of written culture and of literature. Donald McKenzie taught us that the unstable and plural meanings of texts were always dependent on the manner in which they were copied or printed, set out on the page and in the book, recited, read or acted out. He showed that the rigorous analysis of the forms in which texts are published is an essential instrument not only in the task of describing, cataloguing or editing the works, but also in the attempt to understand the intellectual and aesthetic categories which have governed their composition, circulation and use. At a time when semiotic and linguistic schools of criticism read texts without considering the author or their material form, and the social history of culture gave predominance to statistics, McKenzie placed at the centre of his studies the objects and practices which gave meaning to works. Having pioneered this pathway, he was not to tread it alone for long.

He loved the theatre. He was the founder and director of a professional troupe in New Zealand. He devoted a considerable proportion of his research activity to Congreve. An edition of his works which he undertook remains unfinished. This little book, in which Shakespeare, Lope de Vega and Moliere rub shoulders, is published in honour of his work. In fixing on humble objects (a pirate edition of *George Dandin*, an annotated copy of *Hamlet*), in giving due importance to every social actor involved in the process of publishing, in upholding as essential the gap between performance and publication, the stage and the page, it endeavours to remain true to his teaching.

Don was an energetic, lucid, generous man. He will be greatly missed.

Roger Chartier
October 1999

Text as Performance

This first lecture will be devoted to the nexus of relations formed during the sixteenth and seventeenth centuries between the forms of transmission of texts or, to put it another way, the different modalities of their performance, and their possible reception by their different audiences. Such an inquiry has a fundamental objective: to identify the modes of circulation and appropriation of works and genres whose status, function, and usages were not those implied either by printed inscription or by silent and individual reading habits.

The contemporary relationship to literary works and genres cannot be considered either invariable or universal. Against the temptations of any ethnocentrism of reading it is necessary to recall how numerous are the ancient texts which in no way implied, as addressee, a solitary and silent reader, in search of meaning. Composed to be spoken or to be read aloud and shared before a listening audience, invested with a ritual function, thought of as machines designed to produce effects, they obey the laws proper to oral and communal transmission.

I would like to situate this question within the field of interest that is my own and which strives to link the study of texts, whether they be canonical or ordinary, 'literary' or not, the analysis of their material forms and modes of circulation, and the understanding of their interpretations, usages, and appropriations by their different reading and listening audiences.

The aim of such a perspective would be to break with the uncritical posture, often present in literary criticism, which assumes that all texts, all works, all genres have been read, identified, and received according to the criteria which characterize our own relation to the written word. It is thus a question of historicizing the definition and taxonomies of genres, the practices of reading, the forms of destination and the figure of the addressees of texts as they have been bequeathed to us by the 'literary institution'. Confronted with works dating from the XVIth and XVIIth centuries (and *a fortiori* from earlier periods or from non-Western cultures), categories which we use spontaneously ought to lose their assumed self-evidence and universality.

In order to illustrate this point I would like to begin with a poetic detour, a tale- a *'cuento'* as its author Borges writes. It is a 'fiction' entitled *El espejo y la máscara*, published in the collection *El libro de arena*.[1] In it, Borges tells the story of a king and a bard. After having defeated his Norwegian enemy, the High King of Ireland asks the poet Ollan to write an ode that will celebrate his triumph and establish his glory for all eternity. *'Las proezas más claras pierden su lustre si no se las amoneda en palabras [. . .] Yo seré Eneas; tu serás mi Virgilio'* ('The greatest deeds lose their lustre if they are not coined in words. [. . .] I will be Aeneas; you will be my Virgil'). Three times, at a one-year interval each time, the bard comes back before the king with a poem which is the same and yet different. Each time, the poetic writing, the aesthetic which governs it, the form of 'publication' of the text, and the figure of its addressee find themselves modified.

The bard composed his first ode according to the rules of his art, mobilizing all the knowledge which is his: a knowledge of words, images, verse, examples, genres, tradition. The poem is declaimed by its author *'con lenta seguridad, sin una ojeada al manuscrito'* ('slowly, confidently, without a glance at the manuscript') before the king, the court, the 'School of Bards' and crowds of those who *'agolpados en las puertas, no descifraban una palabra'* ('thronging the doorways, were unable to make out a single word'). This first panegyric is a 'monument': it respects rules and conventions, it summarizes all of Ireland's literature, it is set down in writing. Inscribed within the order of representation, it leads one to believe in the exploits of the sovereign. It should thus be conserved and disseminated: the king commands thirty scribes to copy it twelve times each. The bard has been a good artisan who has faithfully reproduced the teachings of the ancients: *'has attribuido a cada vocablo su genuina acepción y a cada nombre sustantivo el epíteto que le dieron los primeros poetas. No hay en toda la loa una sola imagen que no hayan los clásicos. [. . .] Has manejado con destreza la rima, la aliteración, la asonancia, las cantidades, los artificios de la docta retórica, la sabia alteración de los metros'* ('You have given each word its true meaning, and each substantive the epithet given it by the poets of old. In your whole panegyric there is not a single image unknown to the classics. [. . .] You have skilfully handled rhyme, alliteration, assonance, quantities, the artifices of learned rhetoric, the wise variations of metres.') In recompense, the bard is given a mirror, the work of an artisan like himself and which, like the ode of praise, reflects what is already there.

The king, however, remains dissatisfied. Although it was perfect, the poem remained lifeless. It did not produce any effect on souls or on bodies: *'Todo está bien y sin embargo nada ha pasado. En los pulsos no corre más a prisa la sangre. Las manos no han buscado los arcos. Nadie ha palidecido. Nadie profirió un grito de batalla, nadie opuso el pecho a los vikings'* ('All is well and yet nothing has happened. In our veins the blood runs no faster. Our hands have not sought the bow. No one has turned pale. No one uttered a battle cry or set his breast against the Vikings'). The bard deserved a reward, but he must compose another work: *'Dentro del término de un año aplaudiremos otra loa, poeta'* ('Before a year is out, poet, we shall applaud another ode').

One year later, the poet is back before the king. His new poem is quite different from the preceding one. On the one hand, the new ode breaks all the rules, whether they be grammatical (*'Un sustantivo singular podía regir un verbo plural. Las preposiciones eran ajenas a las normas communes'* – 'A singular noun

3

governed a plural verb. The prepositions were alien to common usage'), poetic ('*La aspereza alternaba con la dulzura*' – 'Harshness alternated with sweetness'), or rhetorical ('*Las metáforas eran arbitrarias o así lo parecían*' – 'The metaphors were arbitrary, or so they seemed'). The work in no way conforms to the conventions of literary art; it is no longer imitation but invention.

On the other hand the poet, this time, reads his work. He no longer recites it with the mastery which was his one year earlier. He reads with uneasiness, hesitation, uncertainty: '*lo leyó con visible inseguridad, omitiendo ciertos pasajes, como si él mismo no los entendiera del todo o no quisiera profanarlos*' ('He read it obviously hesitant, omitting certain passages as if he himself did not completely understand them or did not wish to profane them'). This reading takes place before the king and the circle of men of letters, but the public has disappeared. This new text, strange, surprising, no longer belongs to the order of representation but to that of illusion. It does not lead one to believe in the exploits of the king. It *is* these exploits, 'shown' to the listening audience. '*No era una descripción de la batalla, era la batalla*' ('It was not a description of the battle – it was the battle'). The poem gives rise to the event itself, in its original force. *Ékphrasis* has been substituted for representation.

The poem captures and captivates its audience: '*Suspende, maravilla y deslumbra*' ('It astounds, it dazzles, it causes wonderment'). It exerts an effect on one's sensibility which the first ode in no way accomplished in spite of its formal perfection. Borges goes back, in order to characterize these effects, to the very vocabulary which was that of Spanish Golden Age literature: '*embelesar*', '*maravillar*', '*encantar*'. At that time fiction was thought of and condemned as a dangerous enchantment that annuls the gap between the world of the text and the world of the reader.[2] The poet's second ode should be preserved, but it is not destined for the illiterate but, rather, only for the learned, and in small number: '*Un cofre de marfil será la custodia del único ejemplar*' ('An ivory casket will be the resting place of its single copy'). For his creation, which has the force of theatrical illusion, the poet receives an object of the theatre, a golden mask, sign of the power of his invention. Yet the king wants a work still more sublime.

Upon his return one year later, the ode that the bard brings with him is no longer written and it consists of a single line. The bard and the king are alone. The bard utters the ode a first time, then '*el poeta y su Rey la paladearon, como si fuera una plegaria o una blasfemia*' ('the poet and his king savoured it as if it were a secret prayer or a blasphemy'). Everything is turned upside down. The poem is inscribed within the order of the sacred, a prayer or a blasphemy, and it inhabits the poet like an inspired Word. The poet has not respected the rules; nor has he transgressed them. He has been overwhelmed like the Homeric bard or the Greek lyric poet by an inspired word which is not his own: '*En el alba, me recordé diciendo unas palabras que al principio no comprendí. Esas palabras son un poema*' ('In the dawn I woke up speaking words I did not at first understand. Those words were a poem'). Thus inhabited by a language other than his own, the poet became other: '*Casi era otro. Algo, que no era el tiempo, había surcado y transformado sus rasgos. Los ojos parecían mirar muy lejos o haber quedado ciegos*' ('The bard was like another man. Something other than time had furrowed and transformed his features. His eyes seemed to stare into the distance or to be blind.')

Ollan is thus inscribed in the family of blind poets, dear to Borges. In a lecture given in 1977, *La ceguera*, he reminds us that it was at the very moment when he was named Director of the National Library in Buenos Aires, in 1955, that he became aware that he had lost his sight[3] and the famous *Poema de los dones* begins as follows: '*Nadie rebaje a lágrimas / Esta declaración de la maestría / De Dios que con magnifica ironía / Me dio a la vez los libros y la noche*' ('Let no one debase with pity or reprove / This declaration of God's mastery / Who with magnificent irony / Gave me at once books and the night').[4] A librarian and blind, Borges is doubly heir: of the blind librarians who preceded him in his position at the National Library, Paul Groussac and José Marmól, and of the blind poets, inspired in their dark night – Homer, Milton, Joyce.

Murmured, the third ode is an 'event' and not a 'monument'. It was not written; it will not be repeated. It constitutes a unique experience, and there is no possible reading of it. Its mystery leads those who utter it to forbidden contemplation. '*Sentí que había cometido un pecado, quizá el que no perdona el Espíritu*' ('I felt I had committed a sin, perhaps one the Holy Ghost does not forgive') says the poet. And the king replies: '*El que ahora compartimos los dos. El de haber conocido la Belleza, que es un don vedado a los hombres. Ahora nos toca expiarlo*' ('The one we two now share. The sin of having known Beauty, which is a gift forbidden to men. Now it behoves us to expiate it'). The king's third gift is thus an instrument of death: a dagger with which the poet commits suicide. The king's expiation takes another form, one appropriate for the great theatre of the world where roles are ephemeral and interchangeable: '*es un mendigo que recorre los caminos de Irlanda, que fue su reino, y no ha repetido nunca el poema*' ('he is a beggar wandering the length and breadth of Ireland – which was once his kingdom – and he has never repeated the poem').

Borges's fable takes us from the monument to the event, from inscription to performance. It designates with poetic acuteness the different registers of oppositions that organize textuality. These have to do with aesthetic norms (imitation, invention, inspiration), modes of transmission of the text (recitation, reading aloud, saying it to oneself), the nature of the addressee (the public at large, the learned, the prince or, finally, the poet himself), and the relationship between words and things (inscribed within the order of representation, that of illusion or that of mystery). The 'tale' of the mirror and the mask, of the poet and the king, thus provides questions and categories which indicate how to enter into the analysis of the forms of production, circulation and appropriation of texts, while considering their variations across time, place, and community as essential. Clearly, the lesson does not account for the poetic fulguration of Borges' text but it is perhaps faithful to what Borges himself wrote in a preface to *Macbeth*: '*El arte ocurre declaró Whistler, pero la conciencia de que no acabaremos nunca de descifrar el misterio estético no se opone al examen de los hechos que lo hicieron posible*' ('Art happens, declared Whistler, but the idea that we will never have done with deciphering the aesthetic mystery does not stand in the way of our examination of the facts which made it possible').[5]

The opposition I have drawn between the text as 'monument' and the text as 'event' was proposed by a historian of classical literature, Florence Dupont, in a book which underscores the insufficiency of the categories traditionally associated with the idea of literature for understanding the production and circulation of texts in Antiquity[6]. What are these fundamental notions which constitute the 'literary institution'? First of all, the identification of the work with a written text that is fixed, stabilized, and, thanks to its permanence, open to manipulation. Then, the idea that the work is produced for a reader – and a reader who reads in silence, for himself or herself and alone, even if he or she happens to be in a public space. Thirdly, the characterization of reading as a quest for meaning, a work of interpretation, a search for signification. The fundamental genres of Greek or Roman literature show that we must distance ourselves from these three suppositions in order to understand the reasons for their production, the modalities of their performance, and the forms of their reception.

The ode, for example, should not be thought of in the first instance as a 'literary' genre, but as a ritual speech act which takes place within a practice of religious sociability that is essential to ancient Greece, the *symposión*, or banquet of Dionysiac drunkenness. The ode is a song addressed to the gods of the banquet as well as a song inspired by the Muses, of which the singer is but the instrument. Far from being the result of an individual creation, the product of a poetic art, the banquet song manifests the overpowering of the speaker by sacred inspiration. The meaning of the text depends entirely on its ritual effectiveness. It cannot be separated from the circumstances in which the poetry is sung since, by invoking the gods, it makes them participate in the banquet. Irreducibly singular, the text can be neither written down nor repeated. It is a moment of surging forth, it is mystery, it is event.

But it is in Greek Antiquity itself that this poetic, ritual, and singular Word was progressively transformed into 'literature'. During the festivals and competitions accompanying the cults of

7

the city-states or the great panhellenic sanctuaries (such as Delphi or Epidaurus), the song inspired by the Muses becomes a genre which has its rules and whose productions can be classified and judged.

This transformation of a ritual event into a poetic monument has considerable consequences. The most fundamental is the gap introduced between the circumstances of actual enunciation – namely, the poetic competition which seeks to crown literary excellence – and the fictional scene of enunciation in the poem itself which refers back to a vanished situation – that of the banquet where the ode was sung for its ritual function. The primeval enunciation has become a literary fiction. The banquet which it evokes is no longer a Dionysiac *symposión* but an imagined feast. A second effect of the transformation of the ritual poetic word into a literary monument is the necessity of assigning it to an author. For that mythical authors were needed and each genre was associated with one author considered as its founder: Homer for the epic, Anacreon for lyric poetry, etc. The primordial author becomes the guarantor for the genre in which new creations can be inscribed. A third consequence is the possibility (or the necessity) of elaborating a poetics that states the rules. The inspired word that overwhelms the poet who conveys it is substituted by the idea of the work as creation and as labour. That is why it is only with lyrical poetry, Pindar or Bacchylides, that the poem can be first compared to a woven textile, and poetic art to a craft. Never in the *Iliad* or the *Odyssey* is the metaphor of verbal weaving, which is used to designate contests in eloquence, ever applied to the song of the poet which, in fact, is not his but the Muses.[7]

When the production of the text is no longer attributed to the spontaneous irruption of the sacred word, it comes to depend on a correct application and imitation of the rules. This is why, according to Aristotle's *Poetics*, or at least some of his commentators, a tragedy ought to be judged, not on the basis of its theatrical performance, but through its reading, which will measure its conformity to the norms. The opposition between rules and performance as the fundamental criterion for the evaluation of plays provides the foundation for polemical arguments mobilized during the literary *querelles* of the XVIIth century, for example those concerning plays by Lope de Vega[8] or Corneille.[9] They oppose, in fact, the learned, who judge plays on the basis of rules and by reading them, and those (starting with the authors themselves) who consider the effects produced on the audience during the performance to be of prime importance.

From these three features (the disjunction between the actual circumstances of the enunciation and the fictive enunciation inscribed in the text; the invention of founding authors; the formulation of an *ars poetica* stating what the rules ought to be) there follows another one: the written inscription of texts which thus constitutes, by this very fact, a scholarly canon, an object of apprenticeship, and a repertoire from which to draw citations, examples, and models necessary for composing new texts. The trajectory of the Greek world thus takes us from a poetry fundamentally linked to its performance, one governed by the forms of sociability and religious rituals in which it is sung, to a poetry that is governed by the rules of the 'literary institution'. The endpoint of such a trajectory occurs during the Hellenistic period, with the constitution of the Library and the Museum of Alexandria. It was at that time that the fundamental categories which will structure and constrain the order of modern literary discourse, as characterized by Foucault in two famous texts, *Qu'est-ce qu'un auteur?* and *L'ordre du discours*,[10] first emerged: the concept of the work, with its criteria of unity, coherence and fixity; the category of author which assigns literary work to a proper name; finally the commentary, identified with the work of interpretation, which brings meaning to light. The three fundamental disciplines of the 'literary institution' (philology, literary history, hermeneutics) are thus set in place at the close of a trajectory leading from 'event' to 'monument' and they find their formulation in the dream of a universal library.[11]

This detour through Antiquity suggests several lessons which apply as well to the Early Modern period. The first defines the 'literary institution' as the separation of the texts from their ritual functions and their availability for pedagogy, citation, commentary. The second cautions against all forms of anachronism, that is to say, all forms of projecting as universal what are individual experiences, localized in time and space – for example, our own. Readers of Antiquity did not read an ode by Anacreon, a poem by Catullus, or the *Satyricon* as we read them. Their relationship to these texts was governed by the ritual or practical efficacy of works read or heard. They were not necessarily silent or solitary readers, characterized by a hermeneutic position. Whence the importance of a history of reading devoted to stressing the historicity of fundamental morphological differences which affect the signification of what is read. The third lesson reveals a trajectory from the inspired Word to controlled imitation, from the singularity of the speech act to its inscription in writing, from the ephemerality of the poetic performance to the repetitiveness of reading. These displacements which characterize ancient literature are not without parallel in modernity. By going through the same itinerary but in reverse, Ollan, Borges's Irish poet, attests to the lasting nostalgia for a lost orality, for the text as performance.

Whence, for the historian, a difficult problem of method: how to reconstruct modalities proper to the oral delivery and aural appropriation of ancient texts since these are for us, by definition, now mute forms of orality? There are, it seems to me, three main strategies which allow us to confront this difficulty. The first seeks to decipher in literary representations the practices of orality: recitation, song, reading aloud, etc. It is therefore a question of constituting the corpus of these silent forms of orality which certain texts represent through the fiction of writing. This is the case for example with the tale told by Sancho in chapter XX of the First Part of *Don Quixote* in which Sancho recounts a story to his master.[12] The description shows with extraordinary acuteness, which one might call 'ethno-sociological', the gap that separates Sancho's ways of telling a story and the expectations of a reader like Don Quixote. Sancho tells his story by multiplying the repetitions, the relative clauses, the broken sentences; he constantly interrupts his story with references to the situation in which he finds himself with Don Quixote. Don Quixote, on the contrary, expects a linear narrative without repetition, without digression. Cervantes thus stages the absolute gap which differentiates ways of speaking from manners of reading (or listening to reading). Sancho tells his story the way one tells the stories ('*consejas*') in his village. But Don Quixote becomes very impatient upon hearing this manner of telling so foreign to a reader like himself who is used to apprehending texts in a written, stable and fixed form.[13]

In the same manner, in chapter V of his *Propos rustiques*, Noël du Fail stages the way in which a rich peasant, Robin Chevet, recounts some old folk tales before his assembled household.[14] The features that Du Fail retains in order to characterize this recitation are the very ones that Cervantes will use in order to characterize the manner with which Sancho tells his stories – thus the appeals to the audience, the digressions, the paren- thetical remarks, the repetitions, etc. This first path of inquiry, only sketched here, is in no way to be understood as reducing the literary text to documentary status, but it does take into account the fact that literary representations of the practices of orality designate (while displacing them onto the register of fic- tion) the specific procedures that govern such modalities of the transmission of texts.

A second mode of inquiry seeks to gather from the works themselves the 'indicators of orality' such as they have been defined by Paul Zumthor: 'By indicator of orality, I mean any- thing that, within the text, informs us about the intervention of the human voice in its *publication*, I mean in the mutations through which the text passed, once or many times, from a vir- tual state to its current form and henceforth existed in the mind and the memory of a certain number of individuals'.[15] These indicators of orality, deposited within texts, are not representa- tions of oral practices, but implicit or explicit devices that destine the texts for addressees who will read them aloud or listen to them.

They may be indisputable, just as when a musical notation or the reference to an already known tune indicates how a text is to be sung – for example in the *cancioneros* or in the broadside bal- lads.[16] They may be simply probable, as in the case of texts that are addressed to a double audience: those who will read and those who will listen to the text being read to them. In all European languages, a couple of verb pairs marks this double reception: *to read* and *to hear*, *ver* and *oír* or *leer* and *escuchar*, *voir* and *écouter*. Prologues, advices to the reader, chapter titles very frequently indicate this double nature of the addressee and the double circulation of the text.[17]

Other indicators, inscribed within the formal structure of works, may equally suggest the oral destination of texts. A number of works, starting with the greatest, such as *Don Quixote*, are organized in short chapters, perfectly adapted to the necessities of 'oral performance' which assumes a limited time of delivery in order not to tire the audience and to accommodate their difficulties in memorizing an overly complex plot. Brief chapters, which are so many textual units, can be considered units of reading, closed in upon themselves and separate. William Nelson has thus demonstrated how the rewriting of certain works (the *Amadigi* by Bernardo Tasso or the *Arcadia* by Sidney) could be understood as the adjustment of the work to the constraints of reading aloud at a time when this practice was a major form of lettered sociability.[18] The division of the text into shorter units, the multiplication of autonomous episodes, the simplification of the plot are all indicators of the adaptation of the work to a modality essential to its transmission. This is doubtless the case for a number of older verse or prose works – in particular, the collections of short stories where a staged fictive enunciation (which imagines the reunion of several storytellers within an enclosed space) possibly coincides with the real conditions of its circulation (through reading out loud).

A third line of inquiry is more technical and more specific. It is devoted to the transformations of punctuation and begins with the hypothesis that there was a passage from oralized to grammatical punctuation or, as William Nelson puts it, a mutation (which in his view dates from the late seventeenth century) in which an elocutionary punctuation indicative of pauses and pitches was largely supplanted by a syntactic one. Verifying such a hypothesis poses a preliminary difficulty: to whom should we attribute the orthographic and graphic forms of early editions? As Malcolm Parkes wrote: 'Printed punctuation may reflect that of the author, that of the person who prepared copy for the press, that of the compositor, or all three'[19] – and we can add also that of the readers invited to correct the punctuation according to a list of errata or their own judgment,[20] or, sometimes, that of a particular reader who substituted handwritten punctuation for the printed one.

According to diverse traditions in the field of textual criticism, the assignation of punctuation varies widely. As far as bibliography is concerned, graphic and orthographic choices are mainly the work of compositors. The compositors who worked in early printing workshops did not all have the same way of spelling words or indicating punctuation. This resulted in the regular recurrence of the same graphic forms in different quires of a book, according to the preferences or habits of orthography and punctuation of the compositor who set the pages which were put together in the formes corresponding to these different quires. This is precisely the reason why 'spelling analysis' which allows one to attribute the composition of the pages of such and such a sheet or a forme to such and such a compositor constitutes, with the analysis of damaged types, one of the surest methods of reconstructing the actual process of the making of a book.[21] In this perspective, based on the study of the materiality of printed works, punctuation is considered, in the manner of graphic or orthographic variations, as the result, not by any means of the intention of the author who wrote the text, but of the habits of the compositors who set the printed pages.

At a time in which there existed a fundamental 'phonetic, orthographic, and semantic plasticity',[22] the margins of interpretation and decision left to the printers or compositors were very wide. Sometimes the author himself was explicit in leaving to the compositors the responsibility for punctuating the book according to their own judgment.[23] In his *Mechanick Exercises*, Joseph Moxon insisted on the role played by the compositor as a fundamental and necessary intermediary between the author and the reader: 'A good Compositor is ambitious as well to make the meaning of his Author intelligent to the reader, as to make his Work shew graceful to the Eye and pleasant in reading: Therefore if his copy be Written in a language he understands, he reads his Copy with consideration; that so he may get himself into the meaning of the author, and consequently considers how to order his Work the better both in the title Page, and in the matter of the Book: As how to make his Indenting, Pointing, Breaking, Italicking, etc. the better sympathize with the Authors Genius, and also with the capacity of the Reader'.[24] Moxon thus opposed a collaborative conception of the process of publication to authors' frequent complaints that their works were corrupted by the ignorance or negligence of the compositors.

From another perspective, that of the history of language, the essential role in the punctuation of the text is played out elsewhere: in the preparation of the manuscript for composition as practised by the 'corrector', that is to say the copy editor who added capitals, accents, and punctuation marks and who thus standardized the spelling and established typographic conventions, and by the proofreader who, according to Moxon, 'examines the Proof, and considers the Pointing, Italicking, Capitalling, or any error that may through mistake, or want of Judgement be committed by the Compositor'.[25] If they remain the result of a work linked with the printing house, choices relative to punctuation are no longer here assigned only or mainly to the compositorial practices. Sometimes the different stages of copy-editing and proof-reading are the duty of the master printer himself or the more learned and skilful of the compositors. This is the case for example in the first treatise on printing written, directly set and printed in only one copy around 1680 by Alonso Víctor de Paredes. Paredes indicated that the 'corrector' had 'to understand the conception of the author' ('*entender el Concepto del Autor en lo que manda imprimir*') and, following such a conception, to apply the right punctuation in the copy, to make up for the carelessness (the '*descuidos*') of the author, and to correct the mistakes made by the compositor by reading the proof while an apprentice is reading aloud the copy.[26] In England such reading aloud of the copy was sometimes attributed to a person whose special duty it was, called '*collector*' in Latin and 'Reader' by Moxon.[27] But more frequently copy-editing and proof-reading were assigned to clerics, university graduates, or schoolmasters employed by publishers and printers in order that their editions were correct to the greatest possible degree. Paolo Trovato has reminded us how important it was for the Italian publishers of the *Cinquecento* to insist on the 'correctness' of their editions, praised in the books themselves with the expression '*con ogni diligenza corretto*'.[28] Whence the decisive role of the copy editors or proofreaders whose interventions are spread out over several stages of the publishing process: the preparation of the manuscript, the different stages of proofreading, the stop-press corrections made during the printing process, the compilation of *errata* in their diverse forms: corrections made in ink on each printed copy, loose leaves which encourage the reader to make the corrections himself on his own copy, or pages of *errata* added at the end of the book. At every stage of this process the 'pointing' of the text could be enriched or transformed.

The role of copy editors and proofreaders in the graphic and orthographic systemization of the vernacular tongues (including punctuation) was far more decisive than the propositions for the reform of orthography advanced by those writers who wanted to impose an 'oral writing' entirely governed by pronunciation.[29] There is, for example, a wide gap between the moderation of the solutions chosen for their editions by the French printers and publishers of the XVIth century and the boldness of the 'reforms' suggested by the authors of the Pléiade. Ronsard, for example, in his *Abrégé de l'Art poétique françois*, proposed doing away with 'all superfluous orthography' (that is to say, all the letters that are not pronounced), transforming the written appearance of words so that they would be closer to the manner in which they are spoken (as is the case with '*roze*', '*kalité*', '*Franse*', '*langaje*' etc. – thus rendering the q and the c useless), and introducing letters in imitation of the Spanish like ll or ñ so as to fix the correct pronunciation of words like '*orgueilleux*' or '*Monseigneur*'.[30] In the advice that he addresses to the reader as a preface to the first four books of the *Franciade*, Ronsard directly linked punctuation marks and oral reading practices: '*Je te supliray seulement d'une chose, Lecteur: de vouloir bien prononcer mes vers et accomoder ta voix à leur passion, et non comme quelques uns les lisent, plutost à la façon d'une missive, ou de quelques lettres Royaux, que d'un Poëme bien prononcé; et de te suplie encore derechef, oú tu verras cette marque! vouloir un peu eslever ta voix pour donner grace à ce que tu liras*' ('I will ask of you but one thing, Reader: to pronounce carefully my poetry and to accommodate your voice to its passion, and not as some read them, more in the manner of a letter or some Royal edict than of a well-read poem- and I also ask you once again that where you see this mark *!* to raise your voice a little so as to give grace to what you are reading').[31] In England, the same effort to adjust the graphic forms of words to their pronunciation (but not the attempt to reduce the multiplicity of spellings) characterized the different treatises which proposed the reform of orthographic conventions.[32] Their titles indicated it very clearly: John Hart's treatise published in 1569 is entitled *An Orthography, conteyning the due order and reason, howe to write or paint thimage of mannes voice, most like to the life of nature* and William Bullokar's was published in 1580 with the title *Booke at large, for the Amendment of Orthographie for English speech.*[33]

Far from the radical propositions of the reformers, often ridiculed by the playwrights as pedants from Shakespeare's Holophernes in *Love Labour's Lost* to Cyrano de Bergerac's Granger in *Le Pédant dupé*, the practices of publishers and printers, if they preserved some link with oralization, limited innovations to the determination of the length of pauses. Here, the fundamental text is that of the printer (and author) Etienne Dolet, entitled *La Punctuation de la langue françoise.*[34] He defines in 1540 the new typographical conventions which were to distinguish, according to the length of the interruption or its position in the sentence, the '*point à queue*' (or comma), the '*comma*' (or colon), 'which is placed in a suspended sentence and not at all at the endpoint', and the '*point rond*' (or period) which 'is always placed at the end of the sentence'. The same nomenclature had already been proposed in the edition of Olivetan's *Instruction des enfans* published in 1537 in Geneva by Jean Gérard where the '*Table des accents et de poinctz*' distinguished between the '*virgule ou point à queue*', the '*deux points*', and the '*point final*'.[35] Similarly an *Instruction et créance des chrétiens* published in Strasbourg in 1546 listed among the list of the '*Lettres survenantes*' the '*virgule*', the '*comma*' and the '*point*'.[36]

French language dictionaries at the end of the XVIIth century recorded both the efficiency of the system proposed by Dolet (enriched only by the semicolon which indicates a pause of intermediate duration between that of the comma and the colon) and the distance established between the reader's voice and punctuation, formerly considered, according to the terminology of Furetière's dictionary, to be a 'grammatical observation' marking the logical divisions of discourse. In the examples proposed by Furetière in his dictionary published in 1690 he indicated that: '*Ce Correcteur d'Imprimerie entend fort bien la ponctuation*' ('This corrector understands punctuation perfectly well') and '*L'exactitude de cet Auteur va jusques là qu'il prend soin des points et des virgules*' ('The precision of this author is such that he even pays attention to periods and commas'). If the first example normally assigned punctuation to the technical skills proper to the copy editors and proofreaders employed by the printers, the second example implicitly referred back to a common lack of interest on the part of authors concerning punctuation. Moxon alluded directly to that carelessness in his *Mechanick Exercises*: 'By the Laws of Printing, a Compositer is strictly to follow his Copy, viz. to observe and do just so much and no more than his Copy will bear him out for; so that his Copy is to be his Rule and Authority: But the carelessness of some good Authors, and the ignorance of other Authors, has forc'd Printers to introduce a Custom, which among them is look'd upon as a task and duty incumbent on the Compositer, viz. to discern and amend the bad Spelling and pointing of his Copy, if it be English'.[37]

Furetière pointed out, however, that there were some authors who were attentive to the punctuation of their texts. Is it possible to find traces of their '*exactitude*' in the printed editions of their works? Let us take the case of Molière. It would be very risky to attribute to him in too direct a manner the choices of punctuation such as they are to be found in the original editions of his plays since, as has been shown for the 1660 edition of *Les Précieuses Ridicules*, punctuation varies from sheet to sheet, even from forme to forme, according to the preferences of the compositors.[38] And yet, the different usages of punctuation that exist between the first editions of the plays, published shortly after their first Parisian productions, and the later editions allow one to reconstruct, if not the 'author's intention', at least the nature of the implied destination of the printed text.

Molière's reticence concerning the printed publication of his plays is well known.[39] Before *Les Précieuses Ridicules* and the need to forestall the publication of the text, made from a pirated copy and under cover of a *privelège* obtained by stealth, Molière never sent any of his plays to the printers. There were financial reasons for this since, once published, a play could be staged by any theatrical troupe, but aesthetic considerations were also present. For Molière, in fact, the theatrical effects of the play depend entirely on the '*action*', that is to say on performance. With this in mind, we can begin to understand punctuation as one of the possible devices (along with the image and stage directions) which allowed something of the '*action*' to be restored in the printed text and its reading.

Systematically compared to the punctuation adopted in later editions (not only in the XIXth century but also as early as the XVIIIth and late XVIIth centuries), the punctuation of the first editions of Molière's plays clearly indicates its link with orality, either in the sense that it enabled the printed text to be read aloud or recited, or gave the readers who would read it in silence the possibility of reconstructing, for themselves, the timing and the pauses in the performance of the actors. The effect of the passage from one form of punctuation to another on the very meaning of the works is far from negligible.[40] On the one hand, the original marks of punctuation, always more numerous, portray the characters in different ways – thus for example the comma, present in the 1669 edition and suppressed thereafter, after the first word ('*Gros*') in this line of verse from *Tartuffe*: '*Gros, et gras, le teint frais, et la bouche vermeille*' ('Stout, and fat, with blooming cheeks and ruddy lips') (Act I, scene 4, line 233), or the accumulation of commas and capitals which distinguishes the Master of Philosophy's way of speaking from that of the Master of Dance in *Le Bourgeois Gentilhomme* (Act II, scene 3). A similar technique of punctuating the lines of different characters in different ways in order to distinguish them had already been used by Ben Jonson in *Volpone* as shown by the 1607 quarto edition of the play.[41] On the other hand, the punctuation marks of

Molière's original editions give the reader the possibility of remembering or imagining the performance of the actors. For example, in the scene of the portraits from *Le Misanthrope* (Act II, scene 4, lines 586–594), the 1667 edition contains six commas more than the modern editions, thus allowing one to reconstruct how Célimène, that is to say the actress playing the part, must emphasize some words, introduce pauses, or elaborate upon the mimicry. Finally, these original punctuation marks throw into relief words which are charged with a particular significance. While the last two verses of *Tartuffe* do not contain any comma in the modern editions, this is not so in the edition of 1669: '*Et par un doux hymen, couronner en Valère, / La flamme d'un Amant généreux, & sincère*' ('And, with my daughter's hand, reward Valère / For this, a love both generous, and sincere'). The last word of the play, 'sincere', is thus clearly designated as the antonym of the word which figures in the title, *Le Tartuffe, ou l'Imposteur (The Impostor)*. These abundant punctuation marks, which serve to indicate pauses that are more numerous and, generally, longer than those retained in later editions, inform readers how they should read or recite the lines of verse and emphasize certain words, normally given with capital letters which have generally been suppressed together with the commas in the later printed editions.

A second example of the attention paid by some authors to the punctuation of the printed editions of their works is given by La Bruyère. The original pointing of *Les Caractères* (for example in the last edition revised by the author and published in 1696) indicates clearly that La Bruyère conceived of the composition of each of the '*remarques*' as a sole musical phrase unbroken by periods, alternating agitated sequences, the rhythm of which is given by a succession of commas, with longer sequences without punctuation. The text was treated as a score and the punctuation indicated its different '*tempi*'.[42] This modality of textual composition was designed for a particular mode of reading, that is to say the reading out loud of the work, or parts of it, for a selected audience of listeners gathered within the sociability of the '*salon*'. But La Bruyère's punctuation was not the only device which governed the aesthetics and reception of the text. The capital letters used for words within the sentence and not only at the beginning affected the construction of the meaning of the text in various ways. They put emphasis or give dignity to some words and, consequently, to the individuals, institutions or objects they designated.[43] They made these words immediately visible to the reader's eye and suggested to the reader who would read the text aloud that he or she had to detach them by making a pause or raising the voice. These capitals therefore contributed to the visual and semantic effects produced by the forms of the inscription of the text on the page. This is also the case for the italics which were used to distinguish the words or expressions which were the target of the irony or criticism of the discourse, or for the commas or semi-colons used for demarcating the quotations of what had supposedly been said by such or such a character.

The inquiry which I have only sketched here raises several problems of a general nature. The first is that of dating the transition from rhetorical punctuation to grammatical punctuation. Is this passage organized around a single chronological trajectory for which the end of the XVIIth century marks a decisive watershed? Does it follow different rhythms depending on the genre? Or, according to the hypothesis formulated by Philip Gaskell with regard to the 'Maske' of Milton's *Comus*,[44] should we not trace these variations back to the diverse contemporary destinations of different copies of the same text, either printed or manuscript? Or have we to consider with Malcolm Parkes that the balance between 'delineating the rhetorical structure of a period, and drawing attention to the logical relationships expressed by its syntactical structures' has dominated the uses of punctuation from the Renaissance onwards and can be found in different texts published during the same period, or even in different passages of the same printed text?[45]

The second problem concerns the causes for the attempts to restore oral punctuation during the XVIIIth century and the methods devised for conveying this. The case of Benjamin Franklin is, from this point of view, exemplary. By imagining the diverse devices which would enable the role of the public orator to be sustained in the midst of a dispersed population, Franklin strives to reconcile the new definition of public and political space, in the dimensions of a vast republic, with the traditional forcefulness of live speech, addressed to the citizens assembled for deliberation.[46] On the one hand, authors of 'public discourses' are invited, in their writings, to make use of genres most directly linked to orality: proverbs, dialogues, and letters (which belong to the oratory genre). On the other hand, an apprenticeship in reading aloud, which points out the duration of pauses and voice pitches, should become a fundamental element of the school curriculum. Finally, a reform of typographical conventions should make the oralization of texts easier thanks to an 'expressive typography' which plays with italics, capital letters added to certain words, or new punctuation marks (for example, with the introduction into English of the inverted exclamation or question marks typical of Spanish and which, placed at the beginning of a sentence, indicate from the outset how one is to pitch one's voice). By mobilizing these resources familiar to him as a former printer, Franklin tried to bring printed discourse as closely as possible in line with oratorical performance and, by the same token, to allow different orators in different places to duplicate in identical fashion the original discourse. Thanks to reading out loud, thanks to 'expressive typography', the discourse of the 'publick Orator' will be 'reproduced' as if he were 'present' in his very absence. In a manner contrary to Condorcet or Malesherbes, who were distrustful of the passions and emotions engendered by oratorical rhetoric and, because of this, full of praise for Gutenberg's invention,[47] Franklin thought it was possible to surmount an apparently insoluble contradiction: how is one to organize around speech a public space which would not necessarily be enclosed within the confines of the city state of Antiquity?

'If wee offend, it is with our good will. / That you should thinke, we come not to offend, / But with good will. To shew our simple skill, / That is the true beginning of our end.'[48] The faulty punctuation followed by Quince makes him say, in the prologue to the 'Comedy of Pyramus and Thisbe', the very opposite of what he would like to say – and what it would have been suitable to say: 'If we offend, it is with our good will / That you should think, we come not to offend. / But with good

21

will to show our simple skill: / That is the true beginning of our end.' The play of faulty punctuation, which reverses the very meaning of the text, was used on several occasions in Elizabethan literature by playwrights as well as by poets composing 'punctuation poems' whose meaning is changed if the reader respects either the pauses indicated by the commas or the pauses indicated by the periods.[49] Let us recall the 'unpointed' '*Eduardum occidere nolite timere bonum est*' in Marlowe's *Edward the second*. According to the position of the pause after or before '*timere*', the letter given by Mortimer to Lightborne can be understood either as ordering the murder of the king ('*Edwardum occidere nolite timere, bonum est*', that is, according to the translation provided by Mortimer himself 'Feare not to kill Edward, tis good he die') or as saving his life ('*Edwardum occidere nolite, timere bonum est*', that is 'Kill not the King, tis good to feare the worst').[50]

This play with punctuation indicates that the construction of the meaning of texts depends on the forms which govern their inscription and their transmission: 'Meanings are not therefore inherent but are constructed by successive interpretative acts by those who write, design, and print books, and by those who buy and read them'.[51] Against every form of literary criticism or cultural history that considers the materiality of texts and the modalities of their transmission or performance to be without importance, Quince the clumsy and Mortimer the clever remind us that identifying the aesthetic or intellectual effects of meaning produced by textual forms (whatever they may be) is essential for understanding, in their full historicity, the diversity of the reception and the appropriation of texts, whether literary or not.

NOTES

1 Borges, Jorge Luis, 'El espejo y la máscara', in Borges, *El libro de arena*, (1975), Madrid, Alianza Editorial, Biblioteca Borges, 1997, pp. 80–86 (English translation: 'The Mirror and the Mask', in Borges, *The Book of Sand*, Translated by Thomas di Giovanni, London, Penguin Books, 1979, pp. 53–57).

2 Ife, B. W., *Reading and Fiction in Golden-Age Spain. A Platonist critique and some picaresque replies*, Cambridge, Cambridge University Press, 1985.

3 Borges, Jorge Luis, 'La ceguera', (1977), in Borges, *Siete noches*, México, Fondo de Cultura Económica, 1980, pp. 141–160 (English translation: 'Blindness', in *Seven Nights*, translated by Eliot Weinberger, New York, A New Directions Book, 1994, pp. 107–121).

4 Borges, Jorge Luis, 'Poema de los dones', (1960), in *El hacedor*, Madrid, Alianza Editorial, Biblioteca Borges, 1997 (English translation: 'The Gifts' in Borges, *A Personal Anthology*, Edited with a Forword by Anthony Kerrigan, New York, Grove Press, 1967, pp. 194–195).

5 Borges, Jorge Luis, 'William Shakespeare, Macbeth', in Borges, *Prólogos con un prólogo de los prólogos*, (1975), Madrid, Alianza Editorial, Biblioteca Borges, 1998, pp. 217–225.

6 Dupont, Florence, *L'Invention de la littérature. De l'ivresse grecque au livre latin*, Paris, La Découverte, 1994 (English translation: *The Invention of Literature: From Greek Intoxication to the Latin Book*, translated by Janet Lloyd, Baltimore, The Johns Hopkins University Press, 1999).

7 Scheid, John, et Svenbro, Jesper, *Le métier de Zeus. Mythe du tissage et du tissu dans le monde gréco-romain*, Paris, Editions La Découverte, 1994, pp. 117–162 (English translation: *The Craft of Zeus: Myths of Weaving and Fabric*, translated by Carol Volk, Cambridge, Mass., Harvard University Press, 1996).

8 Lope de Vega, 'Arte nuevo de hacer comedias en este tiempo', (1609) in Rozas, Juan Manuel, *Significado y doctrina del Arte nuevo de Lope de Vega*, Madrid, Sociedad General Española de Libreria, 1976, pp. 177–194 (English translation: Lope de Vega, *The New Art of Writing Plays*, Translated by William T. Brewster, New York, Dramatic Museum of Columbia university, 1914).

9 Merlin, Hélène, *Public et littérature en France au XVIIe siècle*, Paris, Les Belles Lettres, 1994.

10 Foucault, Michel, 'Qu'est-ce qu'un auteur?' *Bulletin de la Société française de Philosophie*, t. LXIV, juillet-septembre 1969, pp. 73–104 (repris dans *Dits et Ecrits 1954–1988*, Edition établie sous la direction de Daniel Defert et François Ewald avec la collaboration de Jacques Lagrange, Paris, Gallimard, 1994, *Tome I, 1954–1969*, pp. 789–821) (English translation: 'What Is an Author?', in Michel Foucault, *Language, Counter-Memory, Practices. Selected Essays and Interviews*, edition and introduction by Donald F. Bouchard,

Ithaca and London, Cornell University Press, 1977, pp. 113–138), and *L'Ordre du discours*, Paris, Gallimard, 1970 (English translation: 'The Discourse on Language', in Michel Foucault, *The Archaeology and The Discourse on Language*, translated by A. M. Sheridan Smith, New York, Pantheon Books, 1972, pp. 215–237).

11 Christian Jacob, 'Lire pour écrire: navigations alexandrines', in *Le pouvoir des bibliothèques. La mémoire des livres en Occident*, sous la direction de Marc Baratin et Christian Jacob, Paris, Albin Michel, 1996, pp. 47–83.

12 Cervantes, Miguel de, *Don Quijote de la Mancha*, (1605), Edición del Instituto Cervantes, Dirigida por Francisco Rico, Barcelone, Instituto Cervantes – Crítica, 1998, Primera Parte, Cápitulo XX, pp. 207–22. (English translation: Cervantes Saavedra, Miguel de, *The Adventures of Don Quixote*, Translated by J. M. Cohen, (1950), London, Penguin Books, 1984, pp. 148–160).

13 Moner, Michel, *Cervantès conteur. Ecrits et paroles*, Madrid, Bibliothèque de la Casa de Velazquez, 1989.

14 Du Fail, Noël, *Propos rustiques*, (1548), in *Conteurs français du XVe siècle*, Textes présentés et annotés par Pierre Jourda, Paris, N.R.F., Bibliothèque de la Pléiade, 1965, pp. 620–623.

15 Zumthor, Paul, *La Lettre et la voix. De la 'littérature' médiévale*, Paris, Editions du Seuil, 1987.

16 Watt, Tessa, *Cheap Print and Popular Piety, 1550–1640*, Cambridge, Cambridge University Press, 1991.

17 Frenk, Margit, ' "Lectores y oídores". La difusión oral de la literatura en el Siglo de Oro', in *Actas del Septimo Congreso de la Asociación Internacional de Hispanistas, celebrado en Venecia del 25 al 30 de agosto de 1980*, Giuseppe Bellini ed., Roma, Bulzoni Editore, 1981, Vol. I, pp. 101–123, and *Entre la voz y el silencio*, Alcalá de Henares, Centro de Estudios Cervantinos, 1997.

18 Nelson, William, 'From "Listen, Lording" to "Dear Reader" ', *University of Toronto Quarterly. A Canadian Journal of the Humanities*, Volume XLVI, Number 2, 1976/77, pp. 110–124.

19 Parkes, M. B., *Pause and Effect: An Introduction to the History of Punctuation in the West*, Berkeley and Los Angeles, University of California Press, 1993, p. 5. An identical plurality of interventions (by the compositors, correctors, or authors) is analyzed by Simpson, Percy, *Proof-Reading in the Sixteenth, Seventeenth and Eighteenth Centuries*, London, Oxford University, Humphrey Milford, 1935 (particularly pp. 71–75 for Sir John Harington's translation of Ariosto' *Orlando Furioso* printed by Richard Field in 1591, and pp. 76–79 for Richard Hooker's *Lawes of Ecclesiasticall Politie* printed by John Windet in 1597), and by D. F. McKenzie, *The Cambridge University Press 1696–1712. A Bibliographical Study*, Cambridge, At the University Press, 1966, Volume I, Organization and Policy of the Cambridge University Press, pp. 67–69 and 116–118.

20 See the examples given by Binns, James, 'STC Latin Book: Evidence for Printing-House Practice', *The Library*, Fifth series, Vol. XXXII, No 1, March 1997, pp. 1–27 (examples 32, 33, 35, and 36).

21 McKenzie, D. F., 'Compositor B's Role in the "Merchant of Venice" Q2 (1619)', *Studies in Bibliography*, 12, 1959, pp. 75–89; Hinman, Charlton, *The Printing and Proof-Reading of the First Folio of Shakespeare*, Oxford, At the Clarendon Press, 1963, and Veyrin-Forrer, Jeanne, 'Fabriquer un livre au XVIe siècle', in *Histoire de l'Edition française*, Roger Chartier et Henri-Jean Martin ed., tome 1, *Le Livre conquérant Du Moyen Age au milieu du XVIIe siècle*, Paris, Fayard/Cercle de la Librairie, 1989, pp. 336–369.

22 De Grazia, Margreta, and Stallybrass, Peter, 'The Materiality of the Shakespearean Text', *Shakespeare Quarterly*, Volume 44, Number 3, Fall 1993, pp. 255–283 (quotation, p. 266).

23 Binns, James, *art. cit.*, p. 7 (example 10, M. A. de Dominis, *De republica ecclasiastica*, 1617).

24 Moxon, Joseph, *Mechanick Exercises on the Whole Art of Printing (1683–4)*, Edited by Herbert Davis and Harry Carter, London, Oxford University Press, 1958, pp. 211–212.

25 *Ibid.*, p. 247.

26 Paredes, Alonso Víctor de, *Institución y origen del arte de la Imprenta y reglas generales para los Componedores*, Edición y prólogo de Jaime Moll, Madrid, El Crotalón, 1984, Capítulo X, 'De la corrección, y obligaciones que deven observar, assi el Corrector, como el Componedor, y el de la prensa', pp. 42–45.

27 Cf. Binn, James, *art. cit.*, example 26, p. 15, and Moxon, Joseph, *Mechanick exercises, op. cit.*, p. 247.

28 Trovato, Paolo, *Con ogni diligenza corretto. La stampa e le revisioni editoriali dei testi letterari italiani (1470–1570)*, Bologna, Il Mulino, 1991, and Richardson, Brian, *Print Culture in Renaissance Italy. The Editor and the Vernacular Text, 1470–1600*, Cambridge, Cambridge University Press, 1994.

29 Catach, Nina, *L'Orthographe française à l'époque de la Renaissance (auteurs, imprimeurs, ateliers d'imprimerie)*, Genève, Librairie Droz, 1968.

30 Ronsard, Pierre de, *Abrégé de l'Art poétique françois*, (1565), in *Oeuvres complètes*, Texte établi et annoté par Gustave Cohen, Paris, N.R.F., Bibliothèque de la Pléiade, tome II, pp. 995–1009.

31 Ronsard, Pierre de, *Les Quatre premiers livres de la Franciade* (1572), 'Au lecteur', in *Oeuvres complètes, op. cit.*, tome II, pp. 1009–1013.

32 Masten, Jeffrey, 'Pressing Subjects or, the Secret Lives of Shakespeare's Compositors', in *Language Machines: Technologies of Literary and Cultural Production*, Jeffrey Masten, Peter Stallybrass and Nancy Vickers (eds.), London, Routledge, 1997, pp. 75–107.

33 Cf. Hart, John, *An Orthographie*, 1569, A Scolar Press Facsimile, Menston, England, The Scolar Press Limited, 1969, who stated that 'the writing ought

to represent the severall parts of the voice', and Bullokar, *Booke at large*, 1580, in *The Works of William Bullokar*, Vol. III, Edited by J. R. Turner, The University of Leeds, School of English, 1970.

34 Dolet's treatise is reproduced in facsimile in Catach, *L'Orthographe française à l'époque de la Renaissance, op. cit.*

35 A reproduction of this '*Table*' is given in Baddeley, *L'Orthographe française au temps de la Réforme*, Genève, Librairie Droz, 1993, p. 220.

36 Cf. Baddeley, Susan, *L'Orthographe française au temps de la Réforme, op. cit.*, pp. 342 and p. 438.

37 Moxon, Joseph, *Mechanick Exercises, op. cit.*, p. 192.

38 Veyrin-Forrer, Jeanne, 'A la recherche des Précieuses', in *La lettre et le texte. Trente années de recherches sur l'histoire du livre*, Paris, Collection de l'Ecole Normale Supérieure de Jeunes Filles, 1987, pp. 338–366.

39 Zanger, Abby E., 'Paralyzing Performance: Sacrificing Theater on the Altar of Publication', *Stanford French Review*, Fall-Winter 1988, pp. 169–188.

40 Hall, Gaston H., 'Ponctuation et dramaturgie chez Molière', in *La Bibliographie matérielle*, présentée par Roger Laufer, table ronde organisée pour le CNRS par Jacques Petit, Paris, Editions du CNRS, 1983, pp. 125–141.

41 Graham-White, Anthony, *Punctuation and Its Dramatic Value in Shakespearean Drama*, Newark, University of Delaware Press, and London, Associated University Press, 1995, pp. 122–130.

42 See the two editions which restore the XVIIth century punctuation of La Bruyère's work: La Bruyère, *Les Caractères*, Introduction et notes d'Emmanuel Bury, Paris, Le Livre de poche classique, 1995, and La Bruyère, *Les Caractères*, Présentation et notes Louis Van Delft, Paris, Imprimerie nationale, 1998.

43 See the remarks made by Louis Van Delft whose edition is the first one to restore the capital letters, *op. cit.*, pp. 45–57.

44 Gaskell, Philip, 'Milton, *A Maske (Comus)*, 1634', in Gaskell, *From Writer to Reader. Studies in Editorial Method*, Winchester, St Paul's Bibliographies, 1984, pp. 28–61.

45 Parkes, M. B., *Pause and Effect, op. cit.*, p. 88.

46 Melish, Jacob, *As Your Newspaper was Reading. La culture de la voix, la sphère publique et la politique de l'alphabétisation: le monde de la construction de l'imprimé de Benjamin Franklin*, mémoire de D.E.A., Paris, Ecole des Hautes Etudes en Sciences Sociales, 1992.

47 Cf. Chartier, Roger, *Culture écrite et société. L'ordre des livres (XIVe-XVIIIe siècles)*, Paris, Albin Michel, 1996, pp. 21–26 (English translation: in Chartier *Forms and Meanings. Texts, Performances, and Audiences from Codex to Computer*, Philadelphia, University of Pennsylvania Press, 1995, pp. 9–13).

48 Shakespeare, William, *A Midsommer Nights Dreame* (1600), quoted from Shakespeare, *The Complete Works, Original-Spelling Edition*, General editors Stanley Wells and Gary Taylor, Oxford, Clarendon Press, 1986, p. 372.

49 An example of such 'punctuation poem' is given by Parkes, *Pause and Effect, op. cit.*, pp. 210–211.

50 Marlowe, Christopher, *The troublesome raigne and lamentable death of Edward the second, king of England: with the tragicall fall of proud Mortimer* (1598), quoted from *The Complete Works of Chistopher Marlowe*, Edited by Fredson Bowers, Volume II, Cambridge, At the University Press, 1973, p. 86.

51 McKenzie, D. F., *'What's Past is Prologue'. The Bibliographical Society and History of the Book*, The Bibliographical Society Centenary Lecture (14 July 1992), London, Hearthstone Publications, 1993, p. 18.

II

Copied Onely by the Eare

IN HIS ADVICE 'To the Reader' of the edition of his play *The Rape of Lucrece* published in 1609, Thomas Heywood declared: 'It hath been no custome in me of all other men (courteous Reader) to commit my Playes to the Presse: the reason though some may attribute to my owne insufficiency, I had rather subscribe, in that, to their seveare censure, then by seeking to avoyd the imputation of weakenesse, to incurre greater suspition of honesty: for though some have used a double sale of their labours, first to the Stage and after to the Presse: For my owne part, I here proclaime my selfe ever faithfull in the first, and never guilty of the last: yet since some of my Playes have (unknowne to me, and without any of my direction) accidentally come into the Printers hands, and therefore so corrupt and mangled, (copied onely by the eare) that I have beene as unable to know them, as ashamed to challenge them. This therefore I was the willinger to furnish out in his native habit: first being by consent, next because the rest have been so wronged; in being publist in such savage and ragged ornaments: Accept it courteous Gentlemen, and proove as favourable Readers as we have found you gracious Auditors'.[1]

'Copied onely by the eare': such an expression referred to a practice often evoked and deplored by playwrights in the early modern period. In Spain, Lope de Vega complained about this form of textual theft. In the dedicatory epistle of his *comedia, La Arcadia* published in the thirteenth *Parte* in 1620, he lamented not for the first time the circulation of corrupted editions of his plays and gave this as the reason for printing them despite his reluctance to do so. In this text he described one of the practices that led to the publication of corrupted texts: that is to say, the commerce of '*unos hombres que viven, se sustentan, y visten de hurtar a los autores las comedias, diciendo que las toman de memoria de sólo oirlas, y que éste no es hurto, respecto de que el representante las vende al pueblo, y que se pueden valer de su memoria*' ('these men who live, eat and dress by stealing the *comedias* from the directors of the companies, saying that they are able to memorize them only by hearing them and that this practice is not a theft since the actor sells them to the people and because they can pride themselves on their memory'). Lope deplored such harm caused to the directors of the companies and to the playwrights (the '*ingenios*'). In order to check if these men really possessed such capacious memories as they said they did, Lope has compared his own texts with the transcriptions made by one of them, called '*el de la gran memoria*', the man with a great memory. The result matched his worst expectations: '*he hallado, leyendo sus traslados, que para un verso mío hay infinitos suyos, llenos de locuras, disparates e ignorancias, bastantes a quitar la honra y opinión al mayor ingenio en nuestra nación, y las extranjeras, donde ya se leen con tanto gusto*' ('Reading his transcriptions, I found that for one line of mine, there was an infinite number of his own, full of nonsense, extravagance and ignorance, enough to diminish the honour and reputation of the best poet in our nation and abroad where the *comedias* are now read with so much pleasure').[2] Lope's observation is fully confirmed by the analysis of a manuscript copy of his play *Peribañez y el Comendador de Ocaña* which contains only about a hundred lines in common with the text printed in 1614 in Madrid, Barcelona and Pamplona.[3]

In England, memory was helped by the use of shorthand. We have to recall that at least ten methods of 'characterie', 'brachygraphy', or 'stenography' were published between 1588 and 1626.[4] Thanks to these swift writing systems, the texts of the plays, performed during the afternoon in the public playhouses, could be instantly taken down and then transcribed and sold to a publisher. In the 1637 Prologue of his *If you Know not me, You Know No Bodie; or The Troubles of Queene Elizabeth*, a work dating from 1605, Thomas Heywood alluded to the practice saying that his play 'Grac'd and frequented, for the cradle age / Did throng the Seates, the Boxes, and the Stage / So much; that some by Stenography drew / The plot: put it in print: (scarce one word true) / And in that lamenesse it hath limp'd so long / The Author now to vindicate that wrong / Hath took the paines, upright upon its feete / To teach it walke, so please you sit, and see't'.[5] According to Adele Davidson, evidence for the use of shorthand for the transcription of plays can be deduced from a close comparison of the textual anomalies in the 1608 first quarto of *King Lear* with the rules set out in one of the shorthand systems, John Willis's *The Arte of Stenography* published in 1602. Many of the weird spellings and textual incoherences of the first quarto are only understandable if they are considered as phonetic and aural anomalies introduced by a faulty longhand reconstruction of a shorthand copy.[6] Such an analysis allows us to give new credit to the old hypothesis (abandoned in recent years)[7] which claimed that some of the Shakespearean 'bad' quartos were printed from texts taken down by 'characterie' or 'stenographie'.[8]

In France, the case of the publication of Molière's plays illustrates a similar practice. On July 9, 1661 Molière received a *privilège* for his comedy *L'Ecole des maris*. The official text (printed in the first edition of the play published in August 1661) justified the granting of this royal *privilège* *'parce qu'il serait arrivé qu'en ayant ci-devant composé quelques autres, aucunes d'icelles auraient été prises et transcrites par des particuliers, qui les auraient fait imprimer, vendre et débiter en vertu des lettres de privilèges qu'ils auraient surprises en notre grande chancellerie à son préjudice et dommage'* (because 'some of the plays which Molière had previously composed were taken and transcribed by certain individuals who have printed and sold them to his prejudice and damage under the cover of *privilèges* obtained by stealth from our Chancellery').[9] The text mentioned explicitly the bookseller and printer Jean Ribou as one of the culprits of such piracy and recalled that he was condemned for it by the royal council.

The comedies to which the *privilège* referred were *Les Précieuses ridicules* and *Sganarelle ou le Cocu imaginaire*. The *Précieuses* was the first play that Molière gave to the press in order to forestall the publication of his text based on a pirated copy and under the cover of the *privilège* obtained by Jean Ribou on January 12, 1660 for two 'books', *Les Véritables Précieuses* by Somaize and Molière's play. Informed of such a threat, Molière, in spite of his reluctance to see his plays in print, decided to sell the *Précieuses* to the bookseller Guillaume de Luyne who received a *privilège* for the play on January 19, 1660. This new *privilège* invalidated the previous one and was shared by de Luyne with two other booksellers, Claude Barbin and Charles de Sercy. Molière's play was composed hastily by different compositors working in the same printing-shop and setting the same pages of the text which was published on January 29, 1660.[10] Ribou and Somaize were only able to publish Molière's work put into verse under the cover of a *privilège* dated March 3, 1660. In this first case there is no clear evidence for the origin and the nature of the *'copie dérobée'*, the stolen copy of the *Précieuses* which arrived in the hands of Ribou. It could have been a memorial reconstruction of the play, or a copy of the text made from the authorial manuscript, the prompt-book or a fair copy circulating in Paris. It is impossible to know.

In the case of *Sganarelle ou le cocu imaginaire*, things are clearer. The history of the publication of the play looks at first glance like a banal affair of piracy. On May 31, 1660, Molière had obtained a five-year *privilège* for four plays: *L'Étourdi* and *Le Dépit amoureux*, performed before the *Précieuses* but never published, and two new plays not yet performed, *Le Cocu imaginaire* and *Dom Garcie de Navarre*.[11] But two months later, on July 26, Jean Ribou received a ten-year *privilège* for a play attributed to a certain 'sieur de La Neuf-Villenaine' entitled *La Comédie Sganarelle avec des arguments sur chaque scène* ('with commentaries on every scene'). Under the cover of this *privilège*, Jean Ribou published two pirated editions of Molière's *Sganarelle* in July and August 1660. Molière ensured that the police carried out a search in Ribou's shop, and then, on September 3, that a ban was put on the sale of the pirated editions for a period of five years. Finally on November 16, the Conseil decided to annul Ribou's *privilège* and ordered the confiscation for the benefit of Molière of the one thousand two hundred and fifty copies of the edition printed for Ribou.[12]

But the more interesting part of the story is told by the supposed 'sieur de La Neuf-Villenaine' in a dedicatory epistle to 'Monsieur de Molière, Chef de la troupe des Comédiens de Monsieur'. In this text which repeated ironically some expressions once used by Molière in his preface to *Les Précieuses Ridicules*, the author described the different stages of the transmission of Molière's text.[13] First, he said that he memorized the play after he attended 'five or six' performances of it and that he recited it almost complete in a 'famous company', except for a hundred lines memorized after another visit to the play. Then, he sent a manuscript transcription of the play to a *'gentilhomme de la campagne'*, a 'gentleman in the country'. Since this reader had not seen the play in Paris, La Neuf-Villenaine added to the text *'des arguments de chaque scène'*, 'commentaries on each scene'. Finally, La Neuf-Villenaine indicated that 'eight or ten copies' of the play had circulated in Paris, which had been taken from this transcription in spite of his express desire to the contrary. Whence the ironic conclusion of the dedication. Since many people were quite ready to print the play and in a corrupted form: *'J'ai vu que c'était une nécessité que nous fussions imprimés'* ('I saw that necessity demanded that we should be printed'). Fictitious or not, the story told by La Neuf-Villenaine is quite plausible. It indicates that memorial reconstruction of plays was a practice also known in France even if historians of French literature do not pay much attention to it.

From this arises another question: is it possible to find in some editions traces of this particular form of textual transmission? The Bibliothèque Municipale of Lyons keeps in its collections a copy of an edition of Molière's *George Dandin* without any indication of the publisher or the printer but dated 1669, that is to say, the same year that the first Parisian edition of the play was published by Jean Ribou with whom Molière had by then been reconciled.[14] This copy is a small duodecimo printed on bad paper with a nineteenth century binding identical to other bindings used for a series of plays all belonging to the same collector who was particularly interested in theatrical editions of the seventeenth century. The text given by this edition is a very bad one with the omission of some sentences and many confusions and misprints which make the play sometimes difficult to understand. The absence of many stage directions, in particular in the third act, makes it quite impossible for the reader to understand some of the comical effects produced by a series of cases of mistaken identity.

In spite of or perhaps thanks to the very poor quality of its material production and its text, this copy of *George Dandin* gives us a series of insights into the publication of plays in seventeenth-century France. First of all it throws light on the practice of pirating editions. The title page announces: '*George Dandin / Comédie de Monsieur de Molière*' with only the date, 1669, and no indication of the place of printing or the name of the publisher. But the presence on this title page of an ornament which was Benoît Rigaud's device suggests that the edition was printed in Lyons. It is clearly a pirated edition published as an infringement to the seven-year *privilège* obtained by Molière on September 30, 1668, for two plays *L'Avare* and *Le Mary confondu* – the second is the other title of Molière's *George Dandin* and the only one used by the actor La Grange in the register he kept of the performances and receipts of the company.[15] Under the cover of this *privilège*, Ribou published with the date of 1669 the play as '*George Dandin / ou le Mary confondu / Comédie par J. B. P. de Molière / Avec Privilège du Roi*'. The pirated edition published by Elzevier in the same year 1669 and the one published by an anonymous French provincial bookseller in 1670 are faithful to the text printed by Ribou as they indicate on their title page: '*Suivant la copie imprimée*' or '*Jouxte la copie imprimée*', that is to say, 'according to the printed copy'.[16] But this is not the case for the edition from Lyons which offers a text characterized by numerous differences from the one published in Paris.

This edition, ignored by the bibliographies devoted to Molière's plays, is an example of the publishing strategies adopted by the booksellers in Lyons who were deprived by their Parisian rivals of the possibility of obtaining *privilèges* for publishing the new literary titles. The monarchy preferred to concentrate the *privilèges* in the hands of the members of the Parisian guild who were thus transformed into its clients and it constantly reinforced their monopoly by renewing their *privilèges* once they had expired.[17]

The only weapon against such a confiscation of the more profitable part of printed production was to publish pirated editions or '*contrefaçons*' cheaper than the authorized ones since they were printed on bad paper and with bad ink without any remuneration given to the author. The identification and localization of such editions posed a difficult problem for the booktrade or the legal authorities in the seventeenth century. It remains a tricky problem for bibliographers and historians of the book who try to combine diverse criteria (the form of the signatures and the number of signed leaves in each gathering, the frequency and position of the catchwords, the type of ornaments used) for identifying printers hidden behind anonymity or false addresses.[18] As shown by the pirated editions from Lyons, the problem is rendered still more complex by the imitation on the part of the provincial or foreign printers of the typographical habits of their Parisian colleagues in order to deceive the experts in the trade or the legal authorities. It is occasionally a flaw in this imitation which can reveal the origin of a pirated edition. This happens for example with a 1669 edition of *L'Imposteur ou le Tartuffe* given as '*Sur l'imprimé aux dépens de l'Autheur*' and with Ribou's address. The effort to imitate Parisian practices falls short in two revealing ways.[19] On the one hand, in the gathering 'C' the signatures are used with arabic numerals according to the printing custom in Lyons, not with roman numerals as in Paris and in the other gatherings of the edition. On the other hand, the catchwords appear only at the end of each gathering according to the Parisian custom, except in 'N' in which they are present on the verso of the first two leaves according to the Dutch practice which generally put catchwords on every page. Only a closer analysis could in this case decide if the piracy has to be assigned to a printer in Lyons or to one of his Dutch colleagues. But this example demonstrates that Ribou who pirated two of Molière's plays in 1660 could himself also be the victim of piracy ten years later.

In order to attain a correct understanding of the 1669 edition from Lyons we must recall the different forms through which Molière's *George Dandin* was transmitted. The play was first performed as part of a '*fête*' for the court in the gardens of Versailles on July 18, 1668. It was a moment of triumph for the monarchy. The king, still a young man, played to perfection all the ideal roles of the monarch; with the conquest of Franche-Comté in February, he was a victor in war; with the baptism of the Dauphin in March, he had ensured the dynastic succession, and with the profitable Peace of Aix-la-Chapelle in May, he could be considered as a triumphant peacemaker. The magnificence of the '*Fête*' of July at Versailles was to demonstrate that the king was master of pleasures as he was of armies, that he could offer superb amusements as generously as he granted peace. The theatrical spectacle was only part of this festival which began with a refreshment and ended with a supper, a ball and a fireworks display. The comedy commissioned from Molière was itself intertwined with another comedy in music and ballet which was a kind of pastoral episode recounting the combat of Love and Bacchus. Its text had also been written by Molière and the instrumental music and songs had been composed by Lully. Thus, in its first performance, *George Dandin* was mixed with another dramatic plot and theatrical form and inserted into a multifaceted festive event.[20]

Its second context of performance was the theatre of the Palais Royal which had been given to Molière on October 1661 and which he shared with the *Comédiens Italiens* after that company returned to Paris in January 1662. In this new framework the play was inscribed within the annual calendar of the Parisian theatre season and was performed without the songs and dances. It was presented ten times between November 9 and December 9, each time coupled with another comedy that Molière chose from his repertory either because it was also a new play (*Amphytrion*), or because its plot was also devoted to the anxieties of marriage (*Sganarelle ou le cocu imaginaire, L'Ecole des maris*), or even because the play like *George Dandin* used the resources of farce (*Le Médecin malgré lui*).[21]

The 'same' play was thus given under totally different conditions of representation, each addressed to different audiences (the court or a heterogeneous urban gathering), each mobilizing a specific range of experiences, references, and expectations. In contrast to critical traditions which are indifferent to the ways in which texts are printed or performed and which believe that the significance of a literary work can be fully encapsulated in its linguistic protocols, the dual inscription of *George Dandin* within the court festival and urban theatrical practice reminds us that the meaning of a work depends always on the form in which it is offered to its readers, spectators or listeners. D. F. McKenzie underlined in the Panizzi Lectures he delivered in 1985 that 'forms affect meaning' and that a printed text radically changes meaning by differences in its typographical presentation, its format, the layout of its pages, its illustrations, its organization and divisions.[22] In the same manner the meaning of each of Molière's plays varied quite evidently according to the apparatus of representation that shaped the play to its specific forms.

Is it sufficient to stress that 'with their parasitic absence of function and common cultural ideal, *la cour et la ville* merged into a self-contained, homogeneous society',[23] or to recall the fluidity of the social boundaries between the nobility and the bourgeoisie in order to qualify the difference between the 'court' and the 'city' and presuppose a similar reception of a play by its different audiences?[24] Even if the expectations of the spectators at the court festival and in the Paris hall were the same, the profound differences between the devices governing the two types of performances created a very different kind of relationship to the play. If we accept that the construction of meaning depends in a large part on the forms of transmission and reception of discourses, we have to explore carefully their different effects. Moreover, the horizons of expectations, the shared experiences, or the immediate preoccupations of the courtiers (dominated in 1668 by the reforms of the nobility) and that of the mixed Parisian public (which was far from being only made up of the bourgeoisie) were not at all identical. Consequently what is at stake is the relationship between three elements: the social composition of the audiences, the aesthetic categories and social perceptions that mould the different appropriations of the play, and the diverse modalities of the setting and performances of the text.

But conversely we must consider that the printed forms of the plays are also a kind of 'performance'. The advice to the reader which opened the edition of *L'Amour médecin*, performed at Versailles, then at the Theatre of the Palais Royal in 1665 and published the following year, underscored the gap that existed for Molière between the spectacle and the reading: '*Il n'est pas nécessaire de vous avertir qu'il y a beaucoup de choses qui dépendent de l'action: on sait bien que les comédies ne sont faites que pour être jouées; et je ne conseille de lire celle-ci qu'aux personnes qui ont des yeux pour découvrir dans la lecture tout le jeu du théâtre*' ('There is no need to tell you that there are many things in it which depend on the stage action. It is generally known that plays are only written for performance: the reading of plays is only for those who can imagine the acting of the piece through their reading of it').[25]

In order to reduce the distance between the stage and the page the printed editions of plays could use different devices. First of all, the engravings which formed the frontispieces played a double role. By showing actual or plausible scenery and costumes, they recalled the performances or helped the reader to imagine elements of the 'action'. By choosing one specific scene of the play, the engraving also contributed to fix its meaning as if this dramatic moment summarized the entire plot in one sole image. Indeed, only six plays were illustrated in such a manner during Molière's life but from the edition of 1682 onwards the presence of an engraving before the title page of each play became usual in the editions of his complete works.[26] The second device which was able to convey something of the 'action' within the limits of the printed text is given by the stage directions which enable the reader to imagine entries and exits, the movements on the stage and the acting. Finally, punctuation was another device that allowed the reader to reconstruct in his or her reading, whether aloud or silently, what Molière called in his preface to the edition of *Les Précieuses Ridicules* '*le ton de voix*', that is to say, the tone, pauses and pitches of the actress or actor's voice.

But these different typographical devices could not suppress the acute awareness of the radical distance which existed between the different forms of representation of the 'same' text. Such a distance between the performance and the printed text was expressed by Molière in the preface to *Les Précieuses Ridicules*: '*Comme une grande partie des grâces qu'on y a trouvées dépendent de l'action et du ton de voix, il m'importait qu'on ne les dépouillât pas de ces ornements; et je trouvais que le succès qu'elles avaient eu dans la représentation était assez beau pour en demeurer là [. . .] je ne voulais pas qu'elles sautassent du théâtre de Bourbon dans la galerie du Palais*' ('Since a great part of the graces that were found in them depends on the action and the tone of voice, it mattered to me that they were not stripped of these ornaments; and I found that the success they received when they were performed was sufficient reason for going no further [. . .] I did not want them to jump from the Théâtre de Bourbon to the Galerie du Palais' [that is, the place where the booksellers who specialized in the new literary titles kept their shops]).[27]

But there is also a distance between the performances at the court and the performances in Paris. In the advice to the reader which opened the edition of *L'Amour médecin*, Molière describes differently the nature of the 'lost ornaments' which were linked not with the action on the stage but with the spectacle at the court: '*C'est qu'il serait à souhaiter que ces sortes d'ouvrages pussent toujours se montrer à vous avec les ornements qui les accompagnent chez le roi. Vous les verriez dans un état beaucoup plus supportable, et les airs et les symphonies de l'incomparable M. Lully, mêlés à la beauté des voix et à l'adresse des danseurs, leur donnent, sans doute, des grâces dont ils ont toutes les peines du monde à se passer*' ('It would be desirable that these kinds of works could always be shown to you with the ornaments which accompany them at the king's palace. You would see them in a more bearable condition, and the airs and symphonies of the incomparable M. Lully, mixed with the beauty of the voices and the skill of the dancers, would give them, without a doubt, graces which prove little short of essential to them'.)[28]

The more fundamental distance is the one which opposed the logic of theatrical representation and the principles which governed printed publication. The preliminaries of *Les Fâcheux* performed in 1661 at Vaux-le-Vicomte, Fouquet's château, then at Fontainebleau and the Palais Royal and published the following year, played ironically with the requirements of print.[29] On the one hand, Molière subverted the genre of the dedicatory epistle to the king declaring that if he wrote such a piece '*ce n'est pas tant pour lui présenter un livre que pour avoir lieu de lui rendre grâce du succès de cette comédie*' ('it is not to present a book to His Majesty so much as to have the opportunity to thank him for the success of this comedy') since the king had commanded Molière to add another '*fâcheux*' or character to the play '*qui a été trouvé partout le plus beau morceau de l'ouvrage*' ('judged unanimously to be the most successful part of the work'). While apparently denying that he is writing a dedicatory epistle, Molière was in fact mobilizing the more classical rhetorical figure of the dedication in praising the prince as the primordial source of inspiration, as the first author of the work presented to him. In this sense the king was really an absolute sovereign since he possessed not only what he could give (favours or protection) but also what he received – that is to say, the work offered to him.[30] The other genre mocked by Molière is the commentary or '*examen*' composed by the author himself on his own works: '*le temps viendra de faire imprimer mes remarques sur les pièces que j'aurai faites, et je ne désespère pas de faire voir un jour, en grand auteur, que je puis citer Aristote et Horace*' ('A day will come when I shall print my observations on my plays and I do not despair of showing that, like a great author, I am able to quote Aristotle and Horace'). His target was clearly Corneille who had added commentaries on his plays in the edition of his works published in 1660. What is at stake in this ironic acceptance of the rules proper to printed publication is the process through which the figure of Molière is transformed from that of an actor and director of a theatrical company to a true 'author'.

With the appearance of the *Précieuses Ridicules* Molière became subject to the logic which governs the printing and publication of his plays. The first aspect of such a history is that of the authorized editions of the plays. The mechanism was always the same: Molière asked for a *privilège* to cover one or several plays and then he sold it with the texts to a bookseller or to an association of booksellers acting as publishers. All the plays written and performed by Molière were published in such a manner – except for seven plays which were printed for the first time in 1682, ten years after his death, in the edition of the complete works supervised by La Grange. It is possible to distinguish three stages in the relationship that Molière established with the Parisian publishers for the authorized editions of his plays. Between 1660 and 1666, he collaborated with several of the booksellers who controlled the market for new literary titles, first de Luyne, Barbin and de Sercy, the publishers of *Les Précieuses Ridicules*, and then Quinet, Jolly, Billaine, Loyson and Guignard. Between 1666 and 1670, Molière, by now reconciled with Ribou, gave nine plays to him – among them *George Dandin*. Finally, during the years 1670 and 1671, he began a collaboration with two new booksellers Pierre Promé and Pierre Le Monnier for an edition of four plays. The history of Molière's authorized editions is complicated but by now well known.[31]

The second aspect, the history of the pirated editions, is more complex and obscure. It leads us back to the 'bad duodecimo' of *George Dandin* as encountered in Lyons. A preliminary analysis of the textual differences between this edition and the Parisian edition published by Ribou allows us to identify four types of variants: omissions, substitutions, confusions and additions.[32]

a. *Omissions*. At different moments of the text, part of a sentence is forgotten thus causing incoherence in the syntax and meaning of the text. One example is Dandin's monologue in the first scene of the first act:

—Paris: '*La noblesse de soi est bonne, c'est une chose considérable assurément; mais elle est accompagnée de tant de mauvaises circonstances, qu'il est très bon ne s'y point frotter*' (translated as 'Gentility, as such, is fine, desirable, something you admire, no question about that. But it has too many drawbacks. Stay well out of it!').

—Lyons: '*La noblesse de soi est bonne, c'est une chose considérable assurément: mais qu'il est très bon de s'y point frotter*'. The words '*elle est accompagnée de tant de mauvaises circonstances*' are omitted by the pirated edition.

A second example comes from the dialogue between Dandin and Angélique in the second scene of the second act:

—Paris: '*C'est fort mal fait à vous d'en user comme vous faites. Oui, oui, mal fait à vous; et vous n'avez que faire de hocher la tête, et de me faire la grimace*' (translated as 'you're immoral to abuse it [marriage] the way you do. Yes, immoral. How come you're shaking your head and grinning at me').

—Lyons: '*Cest fort mal fait à vous, et vous n'avez que faire de hocher la tête, et de me faire la grimace*'. All the middle part of the speech, '*d'en user comme vous faîtes. Oui, oui, mal fait à vous*' is forgotten by the pirated edition.

b. *Substitutions*. In different places a line or a word is replaced by different text. A further two examples: the first, from the seventh scene of the third act, involves only a different phrasing of the lines:

—Paris: Monsieur de Sotenville: '*Prenez-y garde, et sachez que c'est ici la dernière de vos impertinences que nous souffrirons*' (translated as 'Make sure you do. This is the last impertinence we'll tolerate from you').

—Lyons: Monsieur de Sotenville: '*Prenez-y garde, et sachez que c'est ici la dernière fois que l'on pardonne à vos impertinences*'

More than simple rephrasing, however, is shown in the second example, from Dandin's final lines in the second act:

—Paris: '*O Ciel, seconde mes desseins, et m'accorde la grâce de faire voir aux gens que l'on me déshonore*' (translated as 'God, help me! Grant me the blessing of letting others see how dishonored I am').

—Lyons: '*O Ciel, secondez mes desseins, et m'accordez la grâce de faire voir aux gens que l'on me fait cocu*' ('Grant me the blessing of letting others see how cuckolded I am').

It is clear that the difference between 'dishonoured' and 'cuckolded' is not without meaning for the aesthetic register of the play.

c. *Confusions*. In many places a word is replaced by another, often to the detriment of the meaning – for example when '*Nous en écouterons davantage* (listen)' is replaced by '*Nous en conterons*

41

davantage (recount)', or '*à cette heure* (hour)' by '*à cette rue* (street)', or '*rude anière* (a word meaning rebuffing)' by '*rude entière*', or '*bien*' by '*mien*', or '*je suis inexorable* (inflexible)' by '*je suis incroyable* (incredible)'.

d. *Additions.* The most important textual variant proposed by the 1669 edition from Lyon is given in the second scene of the first act by the introduction into the dialogue between Dandin and Lubin, a peasant who is Clitandre's servant and emissary, of a series of lines which do not appear in any other edition either authorized or pirated.

—Paris: Dandin: '*Hé? comment nommez-vous celui qui vous a envoyé là-dedans?*'

—Lubin: '*C'est le seigneur de notre pays, Monsieur le vicomte de chose. . . Foin, je ne me souviens jamais comment diantre ils baragouinent ce nom-là. Monsieur Cli. . .Clitande*'.

(translated as:

—Dandin: 'Ah, what's his name, the one who sent you?'

—Lubin: 'He is our local, you know, big man. Monsieur le Vicomte of something. . . Damn me, I can never remember how the hell they say that name. Monsieur Clee, . . . Clit. . . Cleeton').

—Lyons: After Lubin's words '*je ne me souviens jamais comment diantre ils baragouinent ce nom-là*' the dialogue goes on in this manner:

—Lubin: '*Comment appelez-vous ce qu'on prend quand on est malade?*' (How do you call what you take when you are ill?)

—Dandin: *Une médecine* (A medicine)

—Lubin: *Non, ce qu'on prend autre part* (No, what you take elsewhere)

—Dandin: *Un lavement* (An enema)

—Lubin: *L'autre nom* (The other name)

—Dandin: *Comment l'autre nom?* (What do you mean, the other name?)

—Lubin: *Oui l'autre nom de ce que vous dîtes* (Yes the other name of what you say)

—Dandin: *Un clistère* (A clyster)

—Lubin: *Oui, Monsieur Clitandre, cela commence tout de même l'un que l'autre* (Yes, Monsieur Clitandre, they both begin in the same way)'.

This series of discrepancies between the edition from Lyons and the Parisian text cannot be assigned to the usual errors made by compositors: misreading, eyeskip, repetitions, haplography, foul case, or inversions in the setting of the types. Only the omissions of parts of some sentences can be attributed to such compositorial errors. It is thus very unlikely that the edition from Lyons was composed using a copy of Ribou's edition published with Molière's consent in Paris. Another hypothesis must be advanced in order to understand the process of transmission of this pirated text.

The only one acceptable is that of a memorial reconstruction and transcription of the play by someone, another 'sieur de La Neuf-Villenaine' who attended one or several performances of the comedy. Such a hypothesis can be supported by three main arguments. First, the majority of the substitutions or confusions of the edition can be explained only if they are linked to oral transmission either because the text performed, memorized and transcribed was different from the text given by Molière to Ribou, or because the spectator who 'stole' the text made a series of mistakes as he heard or remembered the lines and introduced many anomalies and nonsenses in his transcription. It is not a wrong reading of an already printed text but a wrong hearing of an oral delivery of the play which was responsible for the substitution of words by others often deprived of any meaning in the context of their use.

Another clue to considering this edition from Lyons the result of a memorial reconstruction is found in its title: *George Dandin. Comédie de Monsieur de Molière.* All the other editions published in 1669 and 1670 gave as a title for the play *George Dandin, ou Le Mary Confondu*, the second title being the one mentioned by La Grange in his '*registre*' and by the *privilège* dated September 30, 1668. We have therefore to suppose that the publisher in Lyons was ignorant of this original title (*Le Mary confondu*) and knew only the title of *George Dandin* which could be inferred from the text itself or from the playbills announcing the performances.

A concluding element to support the hypothesis of a text

deriving from a performance is given by the two textual variants I mentioned earlier: the replacement of '*cocu*' by '*déshonoré*' and the dialogue between Dandin and Lubin punning on the resemblance between '*clystère*' and '*Clitandre*'. These two differences from the Parisian and Dutch editions inscribe the Lyons text within a carnivalesque repertoire and the tradition of the farce. It is possible that when Molière gave his play to Ribou, he found these puns and jokes inappropriate. It is possible also that they were improvisations added during the performance or performances attended by the anonymous spectator who memorized and transcribed the text. In any case they indicate that the literary dignity and the authorial status achieved by Molière from 1660 onwards led him or his publisher to suppress or ignore in the printed text of *George Dandin* the kind of jests he used so many times in his first farces and comedies. The logic of the construction and self-fashioning of authorship was also a process of censorship.

The humble example of this 'bad duodecimo' of *George Dandin* can lead us to a more general conclusion. Erasing the different 'semiotic logics' which govern diverse modes of the representation and dissemination of texts always obscures the way such logics affect the construction of meaning. For some approaches to literary texts these differences do not matter. The legal definition of the concept of copyright as it was framed in the XVIIIth century presupposes that the work is always the same, independent of its particular materializations.[33] Aesthetic judgment, which is at the basis of such a legal conception, considers the literary works in themselves, without paying any attention to their different forms, editions or performances.[34] Finally, deconstructionist criticism constructs categories ('archwriting', 'iterability') the aim of which is precisely to overcome the empirical differences between orality and writing, between the singularity of speech acts and the reproducibility of written texts, or between the different modes of inscribing the discourse.

But for the critical and historical approach I have tried to illustrate such differences are decisive if we are to understand what happens when a reader (or a spectator or a listener) encounters a work always given to him or her in a particular form. The legal or aesthetic 'abstraction' of the text which underlies or reinforces the definition of copyright does not account for the process of appropriation the analysis of which requires both the construction of the reader or the spectator as members of specific communities sharing the same abilities, codes, habits and practices, and the characterization of the effects produced by the different modes of transmission and inscription of the texts.

Whence the interest of the faulty and corrupted edition I have presented to you. It allows us to throw light on a way of transcribing plays which has been largely ignored by French literary history. It shows that the modalities of the transmission of theatrical works are multiple and create more textual instability than has traditionally been supposed in the case of the French classical repertory. It obliges us to perceive that the initial historicity of a text does not derive from the circumstances of its production or the diversity of its appropriation, but is inscribed in its materiality itself.

Five years ago, Margreta De Grazia and Peter Stallybrass wrote: 'Formalists call for exacting attention to the minutiae of literary language without giving thought to the printing-house practices that have in modern editions produced them. Historicists, tracing the discursive structures specific to the late sixteenth and early seventeenth centuries, have ignored the extent to which these structures are eighteenth-century constructs. This inattention to textual objects catches both approaches in methodological paradox: formalists closely read printed texts as if they were authorial compositions [or linguistic machines R.C.]; historicists anachronistically read Enlightenment texts as if they were Renaissance discourses'.[35]

A close attention paid to a printed object such as the pirated edition of *George Dandin* I have described allows us to overcome such paradoxes. On the one hand, it reminds us of the diversity of the operations (writing, acting, memorizing, transcribing, composing, printing, etc.) that contribute to the collective production of the text itself. On the other hand, it views the 'negotiation' between the theatre and the social world as not only the purchase of objects, appropriation of languages, or symbolic acquisition of ritualistic or social practices,[36] but also as a negotiation between the different forms of the printed text and its own conditions of transmission and representation.

From the page to the stage, from the stage to the page, what is at stake is not only the circulation of social energy but also the inscription of textual vitality.

1 Heywood, Thomas, *The Rape of Lucrece. A true Roman tragedy*, (1609), in *The Dramatic Works of Thomas Heywood*, London, Volume V, 1874 (quotation from the edition published in 1638, the latest in the author's lifetime).

2 *Las Dedicatorias de Partes XIII–XX de Lope de Vega*, Estudio crítico con textos de Thomas E. Case, University of North Carolina and Madrid, Editorial Castalia, 1975, in *Parte XIII*, 1620, pp. 54–56.

3 Ruano de la Haza, José María, 'An Early Rehash of Peribañez', *Bulletin of the Comediantes*, Vol. XXV, 1983, pp. 6–29, and 'En torno a una edición crítica de *La vida es sueño de Calderón*', in *La Comedia*, Actas reunidas y preparadas por Jean Canavaggio, Madrid, Collection de la Casa de Velázquez, 1995, pp. 77–90.

4 Davidson, Adele, ' "Some by Stenography"? Stationers, Shorthand, and the Early Shakespearean Quartos', *Papers of the Bibliographical Society of America*, Volume 90, n° 4, 1996, pp. 417–449 (particularly p. 422).

5 Heywood, Thomas, *If You Know Not Me, You Know No Bodie or, the troubles of Queene Elizabeth*, (1605), *The Dramatic Works of Thomas Heywood, op. cit.*, Volume I, p. 191.

6 Davidson, Adele, *art. cit.*, pp. 443–449.

7 See against the theory of shorthand transmission of the plays the arguments (now reconsidered) proposed by Duthie, George Ian, *Elizabethan Shorthand and the First Quarto of King Lear*, Oxford, Basil Blackwell, 1949.

8 Commenting on Thomas Heywood's address to the Reader of *The Rape of Lucrece* I have quoted at the beginning of this lecture, Paul Werstine detaches the possibility of memorial reconstruction from the role of the actors: 'Heywood's story not only allows one to keep open the possibility of memorial reconstruction, as do a number of other contemporary stories concerning the printing of sermons, speeches, and plays, but also provides something different from the twentieth century's claustrophobic absorption with actors as the exclusive producers of texts that may have been put together from memory'. See Paul Werstine, 'Narratives About Printed Shakespearean Texts: "Foul Papers" and "Bad" Quartos', *Shakespeare Quarterly*, Volume 41, Number 1 (Spring 1990), pp. 65–86 (quotation p. 84).

9 This document is quoted by Caldicott, C. E. J., *La Carrière de Molière entre protecteurs et éditeurs*, Amsterdam / Atlanta, Editions Rodolphi B.V., 1998, p. 176

10 Veyrin-Forrer, Jeanne, 'A la recherche des Précieuses', in Veyrin-Forrer, *La lettre et le texte. Trente années de recherches sur l'histoire du livre*, Paris, Collection de l'Ecole Normale Supérieure de Jeunes Filles, 1987, pp. 338–366.

11 Cf. Jurgens, Madeleine and Maxfield-Miller, Elizabeth, *Cent Ans de*

Recherches sur Molière, sur sa famille et sur les comédiens de sa troupe, Paris, Imprimerie Nationale, 1963, Document CXXIII, pp. 340–341.

12 *Ibid.*, Documents CXXVI, CXXVII and CXXVIII, pp. 345–351.

13 Molière, *Sganarelle ou le Cocu Imaginaire*, (1660), 'A Monsieur de Molière, Chef de la troupe des Comédiens de Monsieur, frère unique du Roi', in Molière, *Oeuvres complètes*, Textes établis, présentés et annotés par George Couton, Paris, Gallimard, Bibliothèque de La Pléiade, 1971, Volume I, pp. 299–300.

14 *George / Dandin / Comédie /* de Monsieur / de Moliere / M.DC.LXIX (Bibliothèque Municipale de Lyon 805 536).

15 Thuasne, Louis, 'Les privilèges des éditions originales de Molière', *Bulletin du Bibliophile*, 1924, pp. 8–23 and pp. 57–66, Document XIV, p. 18; Madeleine and Maxfield-Miller, Elizabeth, *Cent Ans de Recherches sur Molière, op. cit.*, Document CXCIV, p. 436, and Young, Bert-Edward and Grace-Philputt (eds.), *Le Registre de La Grange (1659–1685)*, Paris and Geneva, Librairie Droz, 1947 (reedition Geneva, Slatkine, 1977), tome I, p. 99.

16 Guibert, Albert Jean, *Bibliographie des Oeuvres de Molière publiées au XVIIe siècle*, Paris, Editions du Centre National de la Recherche Scientifique, 1961 + Supplément, 1965 (reedition 1973), tome I, pp. 283–292.

17 Martin, Henri-Jean, *Livre, pouvoirs et société à Paris au XVIIe siècle*, Genève, Librairie Droz, 1969, t. II, pp. 690–695 (English translation: *Print, Power and People in 17th Century France*, translated by David Gerard, Metuchen N. J., Scarecrow Press, 1993).

18 Cf. Parguez, Guy, 'Essai sur l'origine lyonnaise d'éditions clandestines de la fin du XVIIe siècle', *Nouvelles études lyonnaises*, Genève, Librairie Droz, 1969, pp. 93–130; Sayce, Richard Anthony, *Compositorial Practices and the Localization of Printed Books, 1530–1800*, Oxford, Oxford Bibliographical Society and Bodleian Library, 1979, and Mellot, Jean-Dominique, *L'Edition rouennaise et ses marchés (vers 1600-vers 1730). Dynamisme provincial et centralisme parisien*, Paris, Ecole des Chartes, 1998, pp. 359–366, 378–393, and 571–587.

19 *L'Imposteur, / ou / Le Tartuffe, /* Commedie. / PAR I.B.P. de Molière / Sur l'imprimé aux despens de l'Autheur / A Paris / Chez Jean Ribou, au Palais, vis a vis / la porte de l'Eglise de la Sainte Chapelle / M. DC. LXIX/. Avec privilège du Roy (B.M. Lyon, 264 265).

20 Chartier, Roger, *Culture écrite et société. L'ordre des livres (XIVe-XVIIIe siècles)*, Paris, Albin Michel, 1996, pp. 155–204 (English translation: Chartier, Roger, *Forms and Meanings. Texts, Performances, and Audiences from Codex to Computer*, Philadelphia, University of Pennsylvania Press, 1995, pp. 43–82).

21 Mongrédien, Georges, *Recueil des Textes et des Documents du XVIIe siècle relatifs à Molière*, Paris, Editions du Centre Nationale de la Recherche Scientifique, 1965, tome I, pp. 321–322.

22 McKenzie, D. F., *Bibliography and the Sociology of Texts*, The Panizzi Lectures 1985, London, The British Library, 1986. See also D. F. McKenzie *'What's Past is Prologue'. The Bibliographical Society and History of the Book*, The Bibliographical Society Centenary Lecture (14 July 1992), London, Hearthstone Publications, 1993.

23 Auerbach, Erich, *Das Französische Publikum des 17. Jarhunderts*, München, Max Hueber Verlag, 1933, and 'La cour et la ville', in *Scenes from the Drama of European Literature. Six Essays*, New York, Meridian Books, Inc., 1959, pp. 133–179 (translated into English by Ralph Manheim from the Original German text in *Vier Untersuchungen zur Geschichte der französzichen Bildung*, Bern, 1951, pp. 12–50)

24 Dewald, Jonathan, 'Roger Chartier and the Fate of Cultural History', in 'Forum. Critical Pragmatism, Language, and Cultural History: On Roger Chartier's *On the Edge of the Cliff'*, *French Historical Studies*, Vol. 21, No 2, Spring 1988, pp. 236–240.

25 Molière, *L'Amour médecin*, (1666), 'Au lecteur', in Molière, *Oeuvres complètes, op. cit.*, Volume II, p. 95.

26 Herzel, Roger, 'The Décor of Molière's Stage: the Testimony of Brissart and Chauveau', *The Publications of the Modern Language Association*, Volume 93, No 5 (October 1978), pp. 925–854.

27 Molière, *Les Précieuses Ridicules*, (1659), 'Préface', in Molière, *Oeuvres complètes, op. cit.*, Volume I, pp. 263–264.

28 Molière, *L'Amour médecin*, (1666), 'Au lecteur', in Molière, *Oeuvres complètes, op. cit.*, Volume II, p. 95.

29 Molière, Les Fâcheux, (1662), 'Au Roi' and preface, in Molière, *Oeuvres complètes, op. cit.*, Volume I, pp. 481–484.

30 Chartier, Roger, *Culture écrite et société, op. cit.*, pp. 81–106 (English translation: Chartier, Roger, *Forms and Meanings., op. cit.*, pp. 25–42).

31 See the fundamental studies by Caldicott, C. E. J., 'Molière and his Seventeenth-Century Publishers', *Nottingham French Studies*, Volume 33, No 1, (Spring 1994), pp. 4–11, and his book *La Carrière de Molière entre protecteurs et éditeurs, op. cit.*, 'L'Auteur devant ses éditeurs', pp. 121–149.

32 I compare the text of the play in the edition published by Ribou as it is given by George Couton (*George Dandin*, in Molière, *Oeuvres complètes, op. cit.*, tome II, pp. 463–503), in the 'pirated' edition from Lyons, and in its English translation (*George Dandin or the Confounded Husband*, in Molière, *The Miser and George Dandin*, in new translations by Albert Bermel, New York, Applause, The Actor's Molière, 1987).

33 Rose, Mark, *Authors and Owners: The Invention of Copyright*, Cambridge and London, Harvard University Press, 1993, pp. 73–74, 89–81, 131–132.

34 Woodmansee, Martha, *The Author, Art, and the Market: Rereading the History of Aesthetics*, New York, Columbia Press, 1994, pp. 34–53.

35 De Grazia, Margreta, and Stallybrass, Peter, 'The Materiality of the

Shakespearean Text', *Shakespeare Quarterly*, Volume 44, Number 3, Fall
1993, pp. 255–283 (quotation, p. 256).

36 Greenblatt, Stephen, *Shakespearean Negotiations: the Circulation of Social
Energy in Renaissance England*, Berkeley and Los Angeles, University of
California Press, 1988. pp. 10–11.

III

The Stage and the Page

THROUGHOUT EARLY MODERN EUROPE there was a widespread reluctance to print theatrical plays. The rhetorical formulations of the prologues and advices to the readers multiplied such expressions of the 'stigma of print'. The commonplace is frequent in England. In 1604, John Marston informed the reader of his play *The Malcontent* that 'onely one thing afflicts me, to thinke that Scenes invented, meerely to be spoken, should be inforcively published to be read, and that the least hurt I can receive is, to do my selfe the wrong'. He added: 'But since others otherwise would doe me more, the least inconvenience is to be accepted. I have my selfe therefore set forth this Comedie'. As Molière was to do later, Marston deplored the distance thus created between the lively existence of the play on the stage and its altered form on the page: 'But so, that my inforced absence must much relye upon the Printers discretion: but I shall intreate slight errors in orthographie may be as slightly overpassed; and that the unhansome shape which this trifle in reading presents, may be pardoned, for the pleasure it once afforded you when it was presented with the soule of lively action'.[1]

Two years later, in his address 'To my equal Reader' published in the quarto edition of another play, *Parsitaster, or the*

Fawne, Marston stated: 'If any shall wonder why I print a Comedie, whose life rests much in the Actors voice, Let such know that it cannot avoide publishing; let it therefore stand with good excuse, that I have been my owne setter out'.[2] A second edition of the play was published the same year with this advice on the title page: 'And now corrected of many faults which by the reason of the Author's absence, were let slip in the first edition'. In a new address to the reader, John Marston wrote: 'Reader, know I have perused this coppy, to make some satisfaction for the first faulty impression; yet so urgent hath been my business, that some errors have styll passed, which thy discretion may amend. Comedies are writ to be spoken, not read: Remember the life of these things consists in action'.[3] For Marston, two distinct reasons lay behind the reluctance to print: on the one hand, the process of publication itself that put the work in the hands of the 'rude mechanicals' (as Puck says) who worked in the printing houses and introduced many errors in to the text; and, on the other hand, the aesthetic incompatibility between the natural destination of plays which were written to be acted, seen and heard, and the printed form which deprived them of their 'life'.

None the less the obligation to print was unavoidable. The prologues evoked the diverse reasons used to justify such a decision. The first was the impossibility of preventing the editions of 'stolne and surreptitious copies, maimed, and deformed by the frauds and stealthes of injurious impostors, that expos'd them' as wrote John Hemminge and Henry Condell in their address 'To the great variety of Readers' in the 1623 Folio.[4] The only response for the playwright was to be his 'own setter out'. But other reasons which derived from the conditions themselves of the performances could justify the decision to print. In 1612, John Webster explained to the reader of the edition of *The White Devil*: 'In publishing this Tragedy, I do but challenge to my self that liberty, which other men have tene [taken] before mee; not that I affect praise by it, for *nos haec novimus esse nihil*; onely since it was acted, in so dull a time of Winter, presented in so open and blacke a Theater, that it wanted (that which is the onely grace and setting out of a Tragedy) a full and understanding Auditory'.[5] Paradoxically, the dispersed community of readers will compose the very 'auditory' the play deserved. The traditional opposition between 'auditors' and 'spectators' which designated two theatrical practices (the halls versus the amphitheatres), two publics (the silent learned audience versus the boisterous populace), and two forms of relationship with the works (to hear the text as opposed to seeing the spectacle) is displaced by Webster's characterization of the reading of the play as a form of scrupulous 'hearing'.[6] It is implicitly the same idea found in the remark he made in his advice to 'the judicious reader' published in the edition of *The Devil's Law-Case* in 1623: 'A great part of the grace of this (I confesse) lay in Action; yet can no Action ever be gracious, where the decency of the Language, and Ingenious structure of the Scene, arrive not to make up a perfect Harmony'.[7] Reading is the only way to arrive at a full understanding of this aesthetic perfection and dramatic ingenuity.

Even when the winter is not so dull and the theatre not so dark, the requirements of the performance can alter the plays which were often shortened to fit a convenient running time. From this arose the need to publish them 'according to the true originall copies' as framed on the title page of Shakespeare's First Folio. Sometimes the title page indicated clearly the difference between the play as performed and the play as composed and it suggested implicitly that only the reader through his or her reading would receive the work as it was originally conceived and written. This is the case for example in Webster's *Dutchesse of Malfi* published in 1623. The title page announced: 'The Tragedy of the Dutchesse of Malfy. As it was Presented privatly, at the Black-Friers; and publiquely at the Globe, By the Kings Maiesties Servants. The Perfect and exact Coppy, with diverse things Printed, that the length of the Play would not beare in the Presentment. Written by John Webster'.[8]

The emphasis put upon the act of writing and the importance of reading the plays strongly counterbalanced the 'topos' of the reluctance to print. Such an emphasis was inscribed in the influential legacy of Ben Jonson's attitude. When he published the 1616 Folio of his *Workes*, Ben Jonson broke with traditional practice which transferred the ownership of the plays to the company as if their real 'authors' were the directors of the companies and not the playwrights. By selling his masques and plays directly to publishers, Ben Jonson exploited the resources of the printed book to establish his proprietary relationship to his own writings.[9] In the parodic contract of the 'Induction' of *Bartholomew Fair* he usurped the company's traditional rights by signing an agreement – fictitious of course – directly with the spectators and hearers: 'It is convenanted and agreed, by and betweene the parties abovesaid, and the said Spectators and Hearers, as well the curious and envious, as the favouring and judicious, as also the grounded Judgements and understandings, doe for themselves severally Covenant, and agree to remaine in the places their money or friends have put them in, with patience, for the space of two houres and an halfe, and somewhat more. In which time the Author promiseth to present them by us [that is to say, the actors] with a new sufficient Play called BARTHOLOMEW FAYRE, merry, and as full of noise, as sport: made to delight all, and to offend none. Provided they have either the wit or the honesty to thinke well of themselves'.[10] The theatrical performance was no more thought of as a contribution to a collaborative production of the play but was regarded as a mere vehicle ('by us') for transmitting the author's creation. Such an affirmation of authorship directly linked with the marketplace was not at all exclusive of the patronage system. But the word '*Workes*' used in the title page of the 1616 Folio, which was directly inspired by the 1611 Folio of Spenser's *Works of England's Arch-Poet*, expressed a strong desire to achieve the canonical *auctoritas* of the ancient or consecrated poets and to shape the distinctive playwright's authorial persona by means of the printed book.

Even if authorship continued to be negotiated in relation to collaboration well into the 1660's, the publication of Jonson's Folio and then the publication of Shakespeare's Folio in 1623 opened the path for a profound transformation in the way printed plays were presented.[11] Quarto editions in general highlighted a network of figures associated with the production of the play on the stage: companies, actors, audiences, and the playwrights who revised or developed the original text. After the publication of the two dramatic folios this situation began to change and new publications of plays were more often organized, even in the quarto format, round a central authorial figure whose art could be fully appraised only through the reading of his composition.

An identical tension between the scorn for print and the merits of the published text also characterized the 'comedia' in the Spanish Golden Age. A good example is the edition of the Fourth Volume or 'Parte' of Lope de Vega's plays published in 1614.[12] The editor of the book, Gaspar de Pomes, recalled in its dedication to Don Luis Fernandez de Córdoba that the author 'had no desire to see things printed which he wrote with a very different intention' ['con tan diferente intento']. Lope indicated the fundamental reason of such an aesthetic position in the dedication of his play, La Campana de Aragón: 'La fuerza de las historias representada es tanto mayor que leída, cuanta diferencia se advierte de la verdad a la pintura y del original al retrato [. . .] Pues con esto nadie podrá negar que las famozas hazañas o sentencias, referidas al vivo con sus personas, no sean de grande efecto para renovar la fama desde los teatros a las memorias de las gentes, donde los libros lo hacen con menos fuerza y más dificultad y espacio' ('The power of histories when staged rather than read is greater, just as the difference between reality and a painting or between the original and a portrait is great [. . .] Thus, no-one can deny that famous exploits or utterances, when brought back to life with the characters, will not have the effect of renewing fame in people's memories from the stage, whereas books do likewise but less powerfully and with greater difficulty and at greater length').[13] In this sense the printed publication of a 'comedia' is only the unfaithful, weak, and inert copy of the performance which is its original and truth.

But in spite of the poet's reluctance the 'comedias' were printed and the editor of the Fourth 'Parte' had to justify his decision. In order to do so, he developed three arguments. The first referred to the need to print the plays according to the original copies ('sacadas de sus originales') in order to restore the authenticity of their texts which had been circulated in corrupted editions – 'tan bárbaras' the address to the reader declares.

The second justification alluded to the usurpation of Lope's name and reputation by playwrights, directors of companies and publishers who used his name for selling plays he did not write. The printing of his own plays and the publication of a list of their titles (given, for example, in the two successive editions of his novel *El peregrino en su patria* in 1604 and 1618),[14] will restore his authorship for the '*comedias*' he really wrote and repudiate the other – supposedly bad – plays which were attributed to him and which damaged his honour and reputation.

The editor of the Fourth '*Parte*' added a final argument for printing ('*dar luz*') the twelve plays he published from the original copies: '*Aquí pues verá el Lector en esta doce comedias muchas cosas sentenciosas, y graves, y muchas, agudas, y sutilmente dichas que aunque es verdad que su autor nunca las hizo para imprimirlas, y muchas dellas en menos tiempo que fue necesario, por el poco que para estudiarla les quedaba a sus dueños, no se deja con todo eso desconocer la fertilidad de su riquíssima vena, tan conocida a todos*' ('The reader will see in these twelve *comedias* many sententious and serious things, and numerous others which are acute and expressed with subtlety, and even if it is true that their author never wrote them for the press and more quickly than necessary because the actors had so short a time left to learn their parts, nevertheless it is not impossible to recognize in them the fertility of his very rich inspiration which is so familiar to everyone').[15] The printed edition will enable the reader of the plays to appreciate their stylistic beauties and to extract from them their more useful '*sententiae*' or 'commonplaces', understood in the positive meaning of the Renaissance as general maxims, imitable examples and universal truths.

Against the classic 'topos' of the irreducibility of plays to print, Lope's '*comedias*' were proposed as material for the intellectual technique which characterized the practices of reading and writing during the Renaissance: the commonplace. Written down in commonplace notebooks or 'tables', as Hamlet says, the quotations, examples or maxims extracted by the reader from the texts he read provided him or her with a repertory of '*sententiae*' he could use to generate new discourse.[16] It is this technique of reading that Lope himself recommended to his son in the dedicatory epistle of his play *El verdadero amante*. In this text where he discussed the classical topic of the opposition between '*armas*' and '*letras*', the choice between a military career and literary studies, he wrote: '*Si no os inclináredes a las letras humanas, de que tengáis pocos libros, y esos selectos, y que les saquéis las sentencias, sin dejar pasar cosa que leáis notable sin línea o margen*' ('If you do not choose letters, you must have only a few books but carefully selected, and you must extract from them the '*sententiae*', and not pass over the things you find important without underlining them or writing marginal annotations').[17] These manuscript annotations or markings added to the printed texts themselves indicated the passages that the reader could or should copy in his commonplace notebook.

In order to facilitate the identification of '*sententiae*', some publishers used different typographical devices which designated the lines to be copied or memorized: commas, inverted commas, asterisks, pointing fingers in the margin, or the printing of the text of the maxims and examples in a type different from the one used in the body of the work. The first example of such a practice for the plays is the edition of Seneca's tragedies published by Giunta in Florence in 1506. In France the publishers of the plays by Robert Garnier followed this model at the end of the sixteenth century,[18] and in England many editions of plays (particularly by George Chapman, Ben Jonson and John Marston) marked in one way or another the lines which were regarded as rhetorical amplifications.[19]

Even if there is no edition of Marlowe's *Edward the Second* with marginal marking of the '*sententiae*', this play is a perfect example of the use of the commonplace as the elements or matrix for theatrical texts. They are present, in the first instance, in the form of quotations coming either from Ovid, who was with Virgil one of the two authors most often quoted in the printed commonplace anthologies from the beginning of the sixteenth century until the 1570's,[20] or from Seneca, a common source for many playwrights according to Thomas Nashe who wrote in 1589: 'English Seneca read by candlelight yields many good sentences, as 'Blood is a beggar', and so forth; and if you intricate him faire in a frostie morning, hee will afoord you whole Hamlets, I should say handfuls of Tragicall speeches'.[21] A Senecan '*sententia*' is quoted by Marlowe in the fourth act of his tragedy when Leicester is moved to pity by the royal prisoner: 'Alas, see where he sits, and hopes unseene / T'escape their hands that seeke to reave his life: / Too true it is *Quem dies vidit veniens superbum, / Hunc dies vidit fugiens jacentem.* ('the man whom the new day sees in his pride / is by the day's ending seen prostrate')[22].

Such a quotation also illustrates the second definition of the commonplace understood as rhetorical '*amplificatio*'. Marlowe used such a device for constructing Edward's lines in the first scene of the last act when the king is imprisoned at Kenilworth. Marlowe alternates the two figures of *amplificatio*: amplification conceived of as the expression of a general maxim deduced from a particular situation (for example with the lines 'But when I call to minde I am a king, / Me thinkes I should revenge me from the wronges / That Mortimer and Isabell have done. / But what are kings, when regiment is gone, / But perfect shadowes in a sun-shine day?') or, conversely, amplification as the application of a universal truth to a particular case (as in the lines 'The forest Deare being struck, / Runnes to an herbe that closeth up the wounds, / But when the imperiall Lions flesh is gorde, / He rends and teares it with his wrathfull pawe, / And highly scorning, that the lowly earth / Should drinke his bloud, mounts up into the ayre: / And so it fares with me').[23] Only the readers of printed editions of the plays would be able to fully recognize, appreciate, copy down or memorize these rhetorical figures which govern the composition of the text. It was a strong reason for overcoming the traditional reluctance to print plays.

Conversely, at least in Spain, the conditions of the performance were the more powerful constraints imposed on the writing of plays. Lope de Vega's *Arte nuevo de hacer comedias en este tiempo* shows this clearly.[24] In this text delivered in 1609 in front of the members of a private academy gathered in Madrid by the count of Saldaña, the constraints which had to govern the composition of plays had no reference to the rules and unities required by Aristotle's commentators since Agnolo Segni's *La Retorica e Poetica di Aristotile* published in 1549.[25] Lope's poetics did not follow these principles; it was defined according to the requirements of the performance. The first condition was the acceptable length of the spectacle which dictated the number of '*pliegos*' or sheets of paper the playwright had to write. According to the *Arte*, each act must correspond to four '*pliegos*' and since a 'comedia' is composed of three acts, its manuscript cannot exceed twelve '*pliegos*' '*que doce están medidos con el tiempo / y la paciencia del que está escuchando*' ('for twelve are well suited to the time and the patience of him who is listening').[26]

The term '*pliego*' must be understood as a sheet of paper folded twice, thus making four leaves for each '*pliego*', sixteen for one act and forty-eight for the entire play. The autograph manuscript of the play *Carlos V en Francia*, dated 1604, matches almost exactly such a length, since the text itself consisted of fifty leaves.[27] All the calculations presented by Lope for displaying his prolific genius are founded upon this basic definition of the '*comedia*' which used the material length of the manuscript as a basis for judging the tolerable length of a performance. In the prologue to the second edition of *El peregrino en su patria*, published in 1618, Lope indicated that he had already written 'four hundred and sixty-two '*comedias*' consisting in fifty '*hojas y más*' ('*hojas*' here in the sense of leaves), that is to say, twenty-three thousand and one hundred handwritten leaves or forty-six thousand and two hundred pages.[28] In the first edition printed fourteen years earlier, Lope limited the number of his plays to two hundred and thirty but, in the dedication addressed to his son of *El verdadero amante*, published in 1620, he boasted a total of nine hundred plays . . . .[29]

The requirements of the performance also placed constraints on the dramatic construction of the plays: '*Pero la solución no la permita / hasta que llegue a la postrera scena, / porque, en sabiendo el vulgo el fin que tiene, / vuelve el rostro a la puerta y las espaldas / al que esperó tres horas cara a cara, / que no hay más que saber que en lo que para.*' ('Do not permit the untying of the plot until reaching the last scene; for the crowd, knowing what the end is, will turn its face to the door and its shoulder to what it has awaited three hours face to face; for in what appears nothing more is to be known').[30] In Lope's poetics the unity of time proper to the performance was much more important than the one which had to contain the plot: *'Porque considerando que la cólera / de un español sentado no se templa / si no le representan en dos hora*s */ hasta el Final Jüicio desde el Génesis, / yo hallo que, si allí se ha de dar gusto, / con lo que se consigue es lo más justo.'* ('But, considering that the wrath of a seated Spaniard is immoderate, when in two hours there is not presented to him everything from Genesis to the Last Judgment, I deem it most fitting, if it be for us here to please him, for us to adjust everything so that it succeeds').[31] All Lope's argumentative strategy in the *'Arte'* rested on the opposition between the primacy of the preferences or expectations of the audience [*'el gusto'*] and the precepts of the learned. An apparent contradiction was thus introduced in the text between the absolute legitimacy of the reaction of the popular audience, *'el vulgo'*, and the negative idea that Lope and others had of its capacity to judge: *'Y, cuando he de escribir una comedia, / encierro los preceptos con seis llaves; / saco a Terencio y Plauto de mi estudio, / para que no me den voces (que suele / dar gritos la verdad en libros mudos), / y escribo por el arte que inventaron / los que el vulgar aplauso pretendieron, / porque, como las paga el vulgo, es justo / hablarle en necio para darle gusto.'* ('When I have to write a comedy, I lock in the precepts with six keys; I banish Terence and Plautus from my study that they may not cry out at me; for truth, even in dumb books, is wont to call aloud; and I write in accordance with the art which they devised who aspired to the applause of the crowd; for, since the crowd pays for the comedies, it is fitting to talk foolishly to it to satisfy its taste').[32]

It is not easy to understand how Lope justified before the learned the dismissal of precepts and poetic rules and the importance laid on applause and public success. It is possible to suppose that the need to please the greatest number of spectators led him to gather together the different audiences which composed the public of the *'corrales'* and which was divided and hierarchized according to social condition and gender, within a single category: the category of the *'vulgo'* which did not necessarily designate a 'popular' public but the audience as a whole.[33]

It is also possible to understand the contradiction between the preferences of the vulgar who were incapable of any aesthetic judgment and the poetics of the learned in another way. By giving primacy to the effects produced by the performance on the audience it was possible for Lope to turn back the Aristotelian reference against the learned. It is the strategy followed by the editor of the Fourth '*Parte*' in 1614. He affirmed: '*no hay en España ni preceptos ni leyes para las comedias que satisfacen al vulgo; máxima que no desagradó a Aristóteles, cuando dijo que el Poeta de la fábula había conseguido el fin, si con ella conseguía el gusto de los oyentes*' ('there is no other precept or law in Spain for the '*comedias*' apart from satisfying the vulgar; it is a maxim which is not displeasing to Aristotle when he said that the Poet had achieved his aim if with his fable he has pleased the hearers'). Thanks to this return to poetic authority it was possible to reconcile public success with aesthetic excellence as measured by the effect produced by the text in performance. At the end of his '*Arte*', Lope, once again obsessed by his meticulous textual accounting, recalled that he is the author of four hundred and eighty-three '*comedias*'. He added: '*Fuera de seis las demás todas / pecaron contra el arte gravemente. / Sustento, en fin, lo que escribí, y conozco, / que, aunque fueran mejor de otra manera, / no tuvieran el gusto que han tenido, / porque a veces lo que es contra lo justo / por la misma razón deleita el gusto.*' ('All of these, except six, gravely sin against art. Yet, in fine, I defend what I have written, and I know that, though they might have been better in another manner, they would not have had the vogue which they have had; for sometimes that which is contrary to what is just, for that very reason, pleases the taste').[34]

The primacy given to the effects produced by the performance created an ambiguous distribution of roles between the playwright, '*el poeta*', and the director of the company, '*el autor de comedias*'. We have to recall that in Golden Age Spain, the 'author' was never the playwright (called '*poeta*' or '*ingenio*') but the man who received the license authorizing the company, who bought the plays from the writers, who rented the '*corrales*' where they would be performed and who was responsible for the distribution of the characters, the scenery, the costumes, and the production itself. In his '*auto sacramental*' *El gran teatro del mundo*, written around 1635, Calderón designated God as '*El*

Autor', that is to say, not only as the poet who wrote the human comedy but also as the 'author' who has created the scenery (the world), chosen the actors (mankind), and distributed roles and costumes. Addressing the World, '*el Mundo'*, he says: '*Seremos, yo el autor, en un instante, / tú el teatro, y el hombre el recitante'* (And now it's time that we began – / I the Director, you the stage, the actor Man').[35] Calderón united in the figure of God represented as poet and 'author', the writing of the work and the performance of the play, the text and the spectacle. But in early modern times things were different: among the protagonists of theatrical practice the distribution of the roles was always unstable and often conflicting.

The trajectory we have followed until now has led us from stage to page either by focussing on the different forms of transmission of the texts or by looking at the constraints imposed on the writing of the plays by the requirements of the performance. I would like now to examine the contrary situation leading us from printed page to theatrical performance. I shall do it by analyzing a particular example: the first known printed prompt book of *Hamlet* in the form of an annotated copy of the quarto edition of 1676 belonging to the John Work Garrett Library at Johns Hopkins University.[36] What is particularly interesting in this copy are the traces left in it by different and successive forms of performance of the text. The title page of this edition announced: *The Tragedy of Hamlet Prince of Denmark. As it is now Acted at his Highness the Duke of York's Theatre.* The edition is thus clearly related to the revival of performances of *Hamlet* given by Sir William Davenant's Company, first in its hall of Lincoln's Inn Field and after 1671 in its new theatre at Dorset Garden. Davenant had received a monopoly on *Hamlet* and eight other Shakespearean plays on December 12, 1660 and he probably staged the première of his *Hamlet* on August 24, 1661 when Samuel Pepys saw it for the first time.[37]

A preliminary notice 'To the Reader' contains the following clarification: 'This Play being too long to be conveniently Acted, such places as might be least prejudicial to the Plot or Sense, are left out upon the Stage: but that we may no way wrong the incomparable Author, are here inserted according to the Original Copy with this mark '[that is to say inverted commas printed at the beginning of the line]'. Such a remark and typographical device invites us to distinguish the presence of three layers of text in the printed edition. The first relates to the play as it was published in its longest form since the second quarto of 1604/1605. Indeed Davenant's *Hamlet* was based on the text of the last quarto edition printed before the Civil War – known as the fifth or sixth quarto and published in 1637.[38]

But – and this is a second textual layer – the text as transmitted by the quarto tradition was revised according to the patent granted to Davenant by the Lord Chamberlain on December 12, 1660, which ordered him 'to peruse all playes that have been formerly written, and to expunge all Prophanesse and Scurrility from the same, before they be represented or Acted'.[39] Compared with the text of the last pre-Civil War quarto, the text printed in 1676 shows that the adherence to this injunction led to the omission or replacement of the word 'God', the excision or dilution of oaths, and the transformation of words or expressions that could be considered as indecent or offensive to piety. A second series of alterations concerned the language itself and led to the substitution of current words and expressions for obsolete, archaic and obscure ones, the omission or clarification of mythological and classical allusions, the literalization or toning down of figures of speech and conceits, and the modernization of grammar and metrics.[40] The text printed in 1676 registered all these changes which had probably been carried out during the 1660's.

The third layer present in the 1676 edition is the text as it was performed by Davenant's company with 850 lines cut out of the 3,730 of the quarto. On the one hand, these cuts, which were needed to limit the length of the spectacle to two or three hours, reinforced the alterations made by the rewriting: they deleted allusions to sex or omitted the lines that resembled oaths. On the other hand, they also profoundly transformed the characters who were reduced to more univocal characterization. They shortened or suppressed entirely the sententious, lyrical or narrative passages considered to be undramatic and, even more importantly in the context of the Restoration, they drastically reduced the number of lines given to Fortinbras.[41] This last alteration shifted the meaning of the play from the return to political order thanks to conquest by a foreign sovereign to the revenge of a legitimate prince against the usurper of his throne. The typographical device chosen by the editor or publisher of the edition of 1676 for indicating 'the places left out upon the stage' inverted the traditional practice of printing houses. While at the end of the sixteenth or the beginning of the seventeenth century the inverted commas (among other markings) indicated to the reader the important lines he or she had to remember or copy down, in the *Hamlet* of 1676 the same sign marked out the passages of the text which could be omitted and forgotten.

The three levels of textuality I have distinguished – the work as it was transmitted by the quarto tradition; the alterations introduced into the text by religious and moral censorship and by grammatical modernization; the cuts imposed by Davenant's adaptation – were present in all the copies of the edition of 1676. What makes the copy in the Garrett Library at Johns Hopkins University of particular interest is the presence of many manuscript annotations which transformed the printed edition into a prompt book used for regulating performances. Fifty years ago, James McManaway, who persuaded the Friends of Johns Hopkins University to purchase this copy, identified the author of the annotations as John Ward by means of a comparison of the handwriting on the quarto copy and different documents (a notebook, a letter, several scraps bearing theatrical data) written by Ward and kept at the Folger Library.[42] John Ward was an actor who worked between 1723 and 1742 in London at Lincoln's Inn Field, then in Dublin with the Smock Alley company and the Aungier Street company, and then again in London at Drury Lane. In 1746, he abandoned his career in London and founded a company of strolling players who gave performances over the next twenty-five years in Hereford, Warwickshire, Gloucester, Shropshire, Radnor, Monmouthshire and Brecknock. The company played four nights a week staying sometimes several weeks or even a larger part of the year in the same town. John Ward retired in 1766 leaving his company in the hands of his son-in-law Roger Kemble.

James McManaway dated from the 1740's the handwritten annotations of the *Hamlet* published in 1676. A close and complete study of these marginalia is beyond the scope of my lecture. I should like only to sketch a rough typology of their nature. The most evident annotations are the marginal indications which aimed at controlling the performance. The warning entries indicated the entrances of the different characters some thirty or forty lines before the indication in the printed text of the moment of their presence on stage. The purpose is clearly to warn the actors before they have to enter. The number of these warning entries varies in each of the acts: fifteen are numbered in the first, seven in the second, twenty in the third, eighteen in the fourth and eight in the last one. The whole text was thus organized by the relation established between the *manuscript* marginal indications of the names of the characters who had to enter some time later and a series of horizontal lines crossed by four, five or six vertical strokes which were marked in front of the *printed* indication of the entry of these characters. In the edition of 1676 each act consisted of only one scene ('Act I, Scene I', 'Act II, Scene I', etc.) and in the absence of scene division the lines with strokes structured the play. They are John Ward's devices for making scenes.

Warning entries were also addressed to the musicians who played either for the entries of the sovereigns – the word used was 'flourish' as in the printed text itself – or at the end of each act (except for the fourth) with the marginal indication 'ring', which was also used for the music accompanying the entries of the Ghost in another edition of *Hamlet*, dated 1683, a copy of which was also transformed into a prompt book by the same John Ward.[43] These manuscript marginalia also regulated the material aspect of the performance. They indicated the objects that the actors had to bring on stage. They mentioned the locus of action: for example, the word 'Town' is written in front of 'Act I, Scene I' which suggests the possible use of painted backdrops or, under 'Act V, Scene I'. we encounter the indication: 'Long Trap open, Earth, Sculls and Bones in it'. They organized the scenery: for example the entries and exits of the Ghost are indicated by 'Ghost under the stage' at the end of the first act or 'Ghost Ready at long trap' at the end of the third one.

But Ward's manuscript annotations were not limited to the margins. They were also concerned with the text itself. The most striking of these interventions was a series of important cuts that limited still more drastically than Davenant's adaptation the length of the play. In Ward's version *Hamlet* was two or three hundred lines shorter than the Restoration *Hamlet*. But in shortening the play Ward did not adhere strictly to the cuts proposed by the printed edition. Sometimes he circled and crossed out lines that Davenant had retained; sometimes he preserved lines that Davenant had suppressed. His interpretation of the Restoration text culminated at the end of the play when he eliminated Fortinbras totally from the last scene and attributed to Horatio the concluding lines: 'There cracks the cordage of a noble heart, good night sweet Prince, / And choires of Angels sing thee to thy rest. Take up the bodies, such a sight as this / Becomes the Field, but here shows much amiss'. This new arrangement which suppressed completely the role of Fortinbras led to the omission of the last line of the quartos: 'Go bid the Souldiers Shoot'.

The beginning of Horatio's last line, 'There cracks the cordage of a noble heart' also shows that Ward's adaptation occasionally transformed the text since the same line in the quartos as in the folios is 'Now cracks a noble heart'. But conversely it is clear that in different places he replaced Davenant's modernizations with the text as it was originally printed in the pre-War quartos, by reintroducing the old word order and also whole sentences and lines omitted by the edition of 1676.

It is likely that Ward compared the text of the edition he owned with the text as it appeared in the quartos from 1604 to 1637, in the successive folios (1623, 1632, 1663–64, and 1685), or in the editions of the complete works published at the beginning of the XVIIIth century by Nicholas Rowe (1709), Alexander Pope (1723–5) and Lewis Theobald (1733).[44] Let us take for example Hamlet's 'To be or not to be'. Following the text of the quarto and the folio Ward restored the line 'Is sick with the pale cast of thought' against the altered and abbreviated version of the adaptation which said 'Shows sickled o're with thought'. Following the reading of the quarto, he corrected 'With this regard their currents turn away' that the 1676 edition shared with the folio, by 'turn awry'. Conversely, it is by following the folio that he completed 'Thus conscience does make cowards' with the words 'of us all' omitted by the quarto. But between these two lines he retained in opposition to the double tradition of the quarto and folio the modernized line 'And thus the healthful face of resolution' in place of 'And thus the native hew of resolution'. Ward's meticulous work of collation and adaptation is demonstrated at the end of the second act when he copied from the quarto editions two lines in the dialogue between Hamlet and Polonius before the entry of the Players which had been forgotten by the compositor in the edition of 1676. However, in a second stage of the preparation of the prompt book he decided to suppress them for the performance and he crossed out his own handwritten addition.

A last but important intervention on the text as presented by the edition was the substitution of handwritten punctuation for the printed one.[45] This substitution affects only the role of Hamlet almost as if John Ward was preparing on the printed page the oral delivery of the character's lines. Let us consider the first six lines of 'To be or not to be'. In the quarto of 1676, the punctuation is faithful to the tradition of the previous quartos and reads:

'To be or not to be, [comma] that is the question, [comma]
Whether 'tis nobler in the mind to suffer
The slings and arrows of outragious fortune, [comma]
 Or to take arms against a sea of troubles, [comma]
And by opposing end them: [colon] to die to sleep
No more, [comma]'

The printed punctuation used only six punctuation marks: five commas and one colon. Ward radically transformed this punctuation thanks to the use of five lengths of pauses and the introduction of question marks. The manuscript punctuation which corrected the printed one is the following one:

'To be, [comma] or not to be? [question mark] that is the question. — [period and dash]

Whether 'tis nobler in the mind, [comma] to suffer
The slings and arrows of outragious fortune; [semicolon]
Or to take arms against a sea of troubles, [comma]
And by opposing end them? [question mark] to die –
[hyphen] to sleep — [dash]
No more; [semicolon]'

Only one single punctuation mark is common to the printed edition and Ward's new punctuation. It is clear that the latter is designed for performance. As in musical scores it indicates a complex use of the pauses and it also marks the tone of the voice. Later in the same soliloquy, the printed text indicated: 'To dye to sleep, [comma] / To sleep perchance to dream; [semicolon]'. By modifying the punctuation Ward gave his own interpretation of these lines based upon different pauses and intonations: 'To dye – [hyphen] to sleep — [dash] / To sleep? [question mark] perchance, [comma] to dream; [semicolon]'

The purpose of this cursory analysis of Ward's annotated copy of the *Hamlet* of 1676, which can be defined both as a prompt book and an acting copy, has been to show the complexity of the relationship that existed between the page and the stage. The 'publication' of plays in early modern Europe always implied a plurality of places, techniques and social actors. It implied also a fluid circulation of the texts between writing, performing, hearing, printing and reading. It is this mobility of texts, the meanings of which were always the result of intricate and conflicting interventions, which I have presented in these lectures by means of intertwining case studies, close readings and general reflections, so adhering to the technique of the commonplace so familiar to the playwrights of the sixteenth and seventeenth centuries.

These lectures have also tried to mingle bibliographical analysis, cultural history and literature. This is perhaps a good reason for returning to Borges – to Borges but also to Shakespeare.[46] The first sentence of 'Everything and nothing' published in *El hacedor* reads as follows: '*Nadie hubo en él; detrás de su rostro (que aun a través de las malas pinturas de la época no se parece a ningún otro) y de sus palabras, que eran copiosas, fantásticas y agitadas, no había más que un poco de frío, un sueño no soñado por alguien*' ('There was no one in him: behind his face (even the poor paintings of the epoch show it to be unlike any other) and behind his words (which were copious, fantastic, and agitated) there was nothing but a bit of cold, a dream not dreamed by anyone'). The absence of the I ('there was no one in him') is the reason for the choice of the double career of actor and author. Actor, first: '*A los vein-titantos años fue a Londres [. . .]En Londres encontró la profesión a la que estaba predestinado, la del actor, que en un escenario, juega a ser otro, ante un concurso de personas que juegan a tomarlo por aquel otro*' ('In his twenties, he went to London. [. . .] In London, he found the profession to which he had been predestined, that of actor: someone who, on a stage, plays at being someone else, before a concourse of people who pretend to take him for that other one'). Author, some time after: '*Nadie fue tantos hombres como aquel hombre [. . .] A veces, dejó en algún recodo de la obra una confe-sión, seguro de que no la descifrarían; Ricardo afirma que en una sola persona, hace el papel de muchos, y Yago dice con curiosas palabras "no soy lo que soy"*' ('No one was ever so many men as that man. [. . .] From time to time, he left in some obscure corner of his work, a confession he was sure would never be deciphered: Richard states that in his one person he plays many parts, and Iago curiously says "I am not what I am" ').

That desperate and failed attempt to conquer an individual identity through the fictions of the theatre expresses the supreme greatness of the poet. A greatness which in his misery he shares with God: '*La historia agrega que, antes o después de morir, se supo frente a Dios y le dijo: "Yo, que tantos hombres he sido en vano, quiero ser uno y yo". La voz de Dios le contestó desde un torbellino: "Yo tam-poco soy; yo soñé el mundo como tu soñaste tu obra, mi Shakespeare, y entre las formas de mi sueño estaba tú, que como yo eres muchos y nadie"*' ('History adds that before or after his death he found himself facing God and said: I, who have been so many men in vain, want to be one man, myself alone. From out a whirlwind the voice of God replied: I am not, either, I dreamed the world the way you dreamed your work, my Shakespeare; one of the forms of my dream was you, who like me, are many and no one').

'*Like me*' God says.

Like all of us.

NOTES

1 Marston, John, *The Malcontent*, (1604), in *The Plays of John Marston in three volumes*, Edited from the earliest texts with Introduction and Notes by H. Harvey Wood, Edinburgh and London, Oliver and Boyd, Volume I, 1934, p. 139.

2 Marston, John, *Parisatister, or the Fawne*, (1606), in *The Plays of John Marston in three volumes, op. cit.*, Volume II, 1938, p. 144.

3 *Idem.*

4 Shakespeare, William, *The Complete Works, Original-Spelling Edition*, General Editors Stanley Wells and Gary Taylor, Oxford, Clarendon Press, 1986, p. LIX.

5 Webster, John, *The White Divel*, in *The Works of John Webster, An Old-Spelling Critical Edition*, Edited by David Gunby, David Carnegie and Anthony Hammond, Cambridge, Cambridge Univerity Press, Volume I, p. 140.

6 Cf. Andrew Gurr, *Playgoing in Shakespeare's London*, London and Cambridge, Cambridge University Press, 1987, 'Audiences or spectators', pp. 85–87.

7 Webster, John, *The Devils Law Case, Or When Women goes to Law, the Devill is full of Businesse*, A New Tragicomedy. The true and perfect Copie from the Originall, in *The complete Works of John Webster*, edited by T. L. Lucas, New York, Oxford University Press, Volume II, 1937, p. 236.

8 Webster, John, *The Tragedy of the Dutchesse of Malfy*, in *The Works of John Webster, An Old-Spelling Critical Edition, op. cit.*, p. 467.

9 Loewenstein, Joseph, 'The Script in the Marketplace', *Representations*, 12, Fall 1985, pp. 101–114; Montrose, Louis A., 'Spenser's Domestic Domain: Poetry, Property, and the Early Modern Subject', in *Subject and Object in Renaissance Culture*, Margreta de Grazia, Maureen Quilligan, and Peter Stallybrass (eds.), Cambridge, Cambridge University Press, 1996, pp. 83–130, and Bland, Mark, 'William Stansby and the Production of *The Workes of Beniamin Jonson*, 1615–16', The Library, Sixth Series, Volume XX, No 1, March 1998, pp. 1–31.

10 Jonson, Ben, *Bartholomew Fair*, (acted 1614), Edited by Douglas Duncan, Edinburgh, Oliver and Boyd, 1972, p. 16–17.

11 Masten, Jeffrey, *Textual Intercourse: Collaboration, Authorship, and Sexualities in Renaissance Drama*, Cambridge, Cambridge University Press, 1997, pp. 113–119.

12 *Doce Comedias de Lope de Vega Carpio* / Familiar del Santo Oficio / Sacadas de sus Originales / Quarta Parte / Dirigidas a Don Luis Fernandez de Córdova / Año 1624 / En Pamplona, por Juan de Oleyza / Impresor del Rey de Navarra.

13 *Las Dedicatorias de Partes XIII-XX de Lope de Vega*, Estudio crítico con textos de Thomas E. Case, University of North Carolina and Madrid, Editorial Castalia, 1975 (quotation from *Parte XVIII*, 1623, pp. 203–205).

14 Lope de Vega, *El Peregrino en su patria*, Edición, introducción y notas de Juan Bautista Avalle-Arce, Madrid, Editorial Castalia, 1973, 'Prólogo', pp. 55–67 (quotation and list of titles on pp. 57–64).

15 *Doce Comedias de Lope de Vega Carpio, op. cit.*

16 See the recent works by Blair, Ann, 'Humanist Methods in Natural Philosophy: The Common Place Book', *Journal of History of Ideas*, 53, 1992, pp. 541–551, and *The Theater of Nature: Jean Bodin and Renaissance Science*, Princeton, Princeton University Press, 1997, pp. 49–81 and pp. 180–224; and Moss, Ann, *Printed Commonplace-Books and the Structuring of Renaissance Thought*, Oxford, Clarendon Press, 1996.

17 *Las Dedicatorias de Partes XIII–XX, op. cit.* (quotation from Parte XIV, 1620, pp. 102–105).

18 Cf. Goyet, Francis, *Le 'sublime' du lieu commun. L'invention rhétorique à la Renaissance*, Paris, Honoré Champion, 1996, pp. 605–609.

19 Hunter, G. K., 'The Marking of *Sententiae* in Elizabeth Printed Plays, Poems, and Romances', *The Library*, Fifth Series, Volume VI, Number 3/4, December 1951, pp. 171–188.

20 Moss, Ann, *Printed Common-Place Books and the Structuring of the Renaissance Thought, op. cit*, pp. 85–90.

21 Nashe, Thomas, 'Preface to R. Greene's 'Menaphon'' (1589), in *The Works of Thomas Nashe*, Edited from the original Texts by Ronald B. McKerrow, Oxford, Basil Blackwell, Volume III, 1958, p. 315.

22 Marlowe, Christopher, *The troublesome raigne and lamentable death of Edward the second, king of England: with the tragicall fall of proud Mortimer* (1598), quoted from Marlowe, *The Complete Works*, Edited by Fredson Bowers, Volume II, Cambridge, At the University Press, 1973, p. 73.

23 *Ibid.*, p. 76.

24 Lope de Vega, *Arte nuevo de hacer comedias en este tiempo*, (1609), in Rozas, Juan Manuel, *Significado y doctrina del Arte Nuevo de Lope de Vega*, Madrid, Sociedad General Española de Libreria, 1976, pp. 177–194 (English translation: Lope de Vega, *The New Art of Writing Plays*, Translated by William T. Brewster, New York, Dramatic Museum of Columbia University, 1914).

25 Cf. Rozas, Juan Manuel, *Significado y doctrina del Arte Nuevo, op. cit.*, pp. 87–88

26 Lope de Vega, *Arte nuevo, op. cit.*, lines 339–340, p. 192 (English translation p. 36).

27 Lope de Vega, *Carlos V en Francia*, Edición de Arnold G. Reichenberger, Philadelphia, University of Pennsylvania Press, 1962.

28 Lope de Vega, *El Peregrino en su patria, op. cit.*, p. 64, note 30.

29 Lope de Vega, *Ibid.*, pp. 63–64, and *Dedicatorias de Partes XIII–XX, op. cit.*, p. 105.

30 Lope de Vega, *Arte nuevo, op. cit.*, lines 234–239, p. 189 (English translation p. 32).

31 *Ibid.*, lines 205–210, p. 188 (English translation p. 31)

32 *Ibid.*, lines 40–48, p. 182 (English translation p. 24–25).

33 José María Diéz Borque, *Teoría, forma y función del teatro español de los Siglos de Oro*, Palma de Mallorca, Oro Viejo, 1996, pp. 37–63.

34 Lope de Vega, *Arte nuevo, op. cit.*, lines 370–376, p. 193 (English translation p. 37).

35 Calderón de la Barca, Pedro, *El Gran teatro del Mundo*, Edición de John J. Allen y Domingo Ynduráin, Barcelona, Crítica, Biblioteca Clásica, 1997, p. 5 (English translation, Calderón de la Barca, Pedro, *The Great Stage of the World*, translated by George W. Brandt, Manchester, Manchester University Press, 1976, p. 2). On theatre performances in the *Siglo de Oro*, cf. Josef Oehrlein, *El actor en el teatro español del Siglo de Oro*, Madrid, Editorial Castalia, 1993, pp. 147–174, y Josep Lluís Sirera Turo, 'Espectáculo y representación. Los actores. El público. Estado de la cuestión', in *La Comedia*, Actas reunidas y preparadas por Jean Canavaggio, Madrid, Collection de la Casa de Velázquez, 1995, pp. 115–129.

36 *The / Tragedy / of / Hamlet / Prince of Denmark. /* As it is now Acted at his Highness the / Duke of York's Theatre / By / William Shakespeare. / London / Printed by Andr. Clark, for J. Martyn, and H. Herringman, / at the Bell in St. Paul's Church-Yard, and at the Blue / Anchor in the Lower Walk of the New Exchange, 1676 (Garrett PO 2807. A2 1676).

37 Spencer, Hazelton, 'Hamlet under the Restoration', *Publications of the Modern Language Association,* Volume 38, 1923, pp. 770–791, and his book *Shakespeare Improved. The Restoration Versions in Quarto and on the Stage*, Cambridge, Mass., Harvard University Press, 1927, pp. 62–110 (particularly pp. 66–70). See also Taylor, Gary, *Reinventing Shakespeare: A Cultural History from the Restoration to the Present*, Oxford, Oxford University Press, 1989, pp. 7–51 (particularly pp. 46–51), and Dobson, Michael, *The Making of the National Poet: Shakespeare, Adaptation, and Authorship, 1660–1769*, Oxford, Clarendon Press, 1992, pp. 17–61.

38 *The Tragedy / of Hamlet / Prince of Denmark /* Newly imprinted and inlarged / according to the true and perfect Copy last Printed / By William Shakespeare / London/ Printed by R. Young for John Smethwicke / and are to be sold at his Shope in Saint Dunstons Churchyard in Fleet-Street Under the Diall / 1637.

39 Radaddi, Mongi, *Davenant's Adaptations of Shakespeare*, Uppsala, Acta Universitatis Upsaliensis, 1979 (quotation p. 67).

40 Spencer, Hazelton, *Shakespeare Improved, op. cit.*, pp. 174–187, and Radaddi,

Mongi, *Davenant's Adaptations of Shakespeare, op. cit.*, 'The Language', pp. 49–63.

41 Radaddi, Mongi, *Davenant's Adaptations of Shakespeare, op. cit.*, 'Cutting: Hamlet', pp. 64–78.

42 McManaway, James G., 'The Two Earliest Prompt Books of *Hamlet*', *The Papers of the Bibliographical Society of America*, Volume 43, 1949, pp. 288–320.

43 *Ibid.*, p. 317.

44 I have compared the texts of the 1637 Quarto and the 1623 and 1664 Folios in the copies of the editions owned by the Lilly Library at Indiana University at Bloomington. For the editions of the beginning the XVIIIth century, see Taylor, Gary, *Reinventing Shakespeare, op. cit.*, pp. 52–99, Dobson, Michael, *The Making of the National Poet, op. cit.*, pp. 117–133, and De Grazia, Margreta, *Shakespeare Verbatim: The Reproduction of Authenticity and the 1790 Apparatus*, Oxford, Clarendon Press, 1991.

45 See on the Elizabethan punctuation of plays the pioneering studies by Simpson, Percy, *Shakespearian Punctuation*, Oxford, At the Clarendon Press, 1911 (who asked the question 'Is it possible to attach a significance to the commas?', p. 8) and by McDonald Alden, Raymond, 'The Punctuation of Shakespeare's Printers', *Publications of the Modern Language Association of America*, Volume XXXIX, 1924, pp. 557–580, and the book by Graham-White, Anthony, *Punctuation and Its Dramatic Value in Shakespearean Drama*, Newark, University of Delaware Press, and London, Associated University Press, 1995.

46 Borges, Jorge Luis, 'Everything and Nothing', (1960), in Borges, *El hacedor*, Madrid, Alianza Editorial, Biblioteca Borges, 1997, pp. 52–55 (English translation: 'Everything and Nothing', Borges, *A Personal Anthology*, Edited and with a Foreword by Anthony Kerrigan, New York, Grove Press, 1967, pp. 115–117).